EDC Providers in Pharmaceutical Industry

Compiled by **Alexandre Jouikov, Ph.D., D.Sc.**

AA Biosciences Inc.
Toronto

EDC Providers

EDC Providers in Pharmaceutical Industry

ISBN 978-0-9812857-0-2

EDC Providers

CONTENTS

Preface

Electronic data capture (EDC) is a current trend in clinical data management. More and more sponsors and contract research organizations (CROs), involved in investigations of new experimental drugs and medical devices move from traditional paper based data collection forms to collecting study information directly in electronic form, using different technologies. There are varieties of approaches around, from collecting information on stand alone PDF forms and sending it for data aquisition to central collecting facility, to numerous automated databases, providing electronic data collection instruments via Internet or via direct connection to database servers.

  This book groups providers of EDC services per country and allows to find a proper vendor close to sponsor or CRO, or close to research sites, if necessary. Each entry briefly lists EDC products, used by the vendor and its EDC services, such as EDC itself (ability to provide on-line access to the study database for data collection and data management), eDiary - electronic patient diaries, ePRO - electronic patient recorded outcome (questionnaires, etc.), IVRS - interactive voice record service, and ability to maintain information, collected via stand alone mobile devices.

Argentina

EDC Providers

Country: **Argentina**

Chiltern International Limited

EDC Products: Not specified

Services:

EDC:	Yes
eDiary/ePRO:	N/A
IVRS:	N/A
Mobile Devices:	N/A

Web Site: http://www2.chiltern.com/

Mailing Address: Saravi Street, B. Los Fresnos 34, Pilar, Buenos Aires, 1629, Argentina

Telephone 1: +54 23 2266 8594

Telephone 2: N/A

Fax: +54 23 2266 8594

Email: N/A

Country: **Argentina**

ICON Clinical Research

EDC Products: Medidata Rave™

Services:

EDC: Yes

eDiary/ePRO: N/A

IVRS: N/A

Mobile Devices: N/A

Web Site: htpp://www.iconclinical.com/

Mailing Address: Av. Fondo de la Legua 143 (B1609JEB), San Isidro, Pcia. de Buenos Aires, Argentina

Telephone 1: +54 11 4006 2222

Telephone 2: N/A

Fax: +54 11 4006 2220

Email: info@iconaus.com.au

Country: **Argentina**

PPD

EDC Products: Acceliant eClinical Suite, Oracle Clinical Remote Data Capture

Services:

EDC: Yes

eDiary/ePRO: N/A

IVRS: Yes

Mobile Devices: N/A

Web Site: http://www.ppdi.com/

Mailing Address: 1300 Maipú St., Piso 15, C1006ACT Buenos Aires, Republica de Argentina

Telephone 1: +54 11 4310 7800

Telephone 2: N/A

Fax: +54 11 4893 3330

Email: N/A

Country: **Argentina**

StudyBuilder AR

EDC Products: StudyBuilder

Services:

EDC:	Yes
eDiary/ePRO:	Yes
IVRS:	N/A
Mobile Devices:	Yes

Web Site: www.studybuilder.com/ar

Mailing Address: N/A

Telephone 1: +44 18 6533 8092

Telephone 2: N/A

Fax: +44 18 6533 8100

Email: ar@studybuilder.com

EDC Providers

Country: **Argentina**

Australia

Country: **Australia**

Adobe Systems Pty. Ltd.

EDC Products: Adobe LiveCycle ES

Services:

EDC:	Yes
eDiary/ePRO:	N/A
IVRS:	N/A
Mobile Devices:	N/A

Web Site:
    http://www.adobe.com/lifesciences/solutions/livecycle/

Mailing Address: Level 4, 67 Albert Avenue, Chatswood, NSW 2067, Australia

Telephone 1: +61 2 9778 4100

Telephone 2: N/A

Fax: +61 2 9778 4190

Email: Use website for communication

Country: **Australia**

ClinPhone

EDC Products: Combined EDC-IVR: DataLabs by ClinPhone (EDC/CDMS) and ClinPhone IVR/IWR

Services:

EDC:	Yes
eDiary/ePRO:	N/A
IVRS:	Yes
Mobile Devices:	N/A

Web Site: http://www.clinphone.com

Mailing Address: Level 50, 120 Collins Street, Melbourne VIC 3000, Australia

Telephone 1: +61 3 9225 5253

Telephone 2: N/A

Fax: +61 3 9225 5050

Email: info@clinphone.com

Country: **Australia**

ICON Clinical Research

EDC Products: Medidata Rave™

Services:

EDC:	Yes
eDiary/ePRO:	N/A
IVRS:	N/A
Mobile Devices:	N/A

Web Site: htpp://www.iconclinical.com/

Mailing Address: Suite 201, Level 2, 2-4 Lyon Park Rd, North Ryde, NSW 2113, Australia

Telephone 1: +61 2 9859 3900

Telephone 2: N/A

Fax: +61 2 9859 3999

Email: info@iconaus.com.au

EDC Providers

Country: **Australia**

Phase Forward Pty Limited

<u>EDC Products:</u> InForm™, Clintrial™, WebSDM™

<u>Services:</u>

EDC: Yes

eDiary/ePRO: N/A

IVRS: N/A

Mobile Devices: N/A

<u>Web Site:</u> http://www.phaseforward.com

<u>Mailing Address:</u> 1 Central Ave, Australian Technology Park, Eveleigh, NSW 1430, Australia

<u>Telephone 1:</u> +61 2 9690 2425

<u>Telephone 2:</u> N/A

<u>Fax:</u> +61 2 9690 1389

<u>Email:</u> info.australia@phaseforward.com

Country: **Australia**

PPD

EDC Products: Acceliant eClinical Suite, Oracle Clinical Remote Data Capture

Services:

EDC:	Yes
eDiary/ePRO:	N/A
IVRS:	Yes
Mobile Devices:	N/A

Web Site: http://www.ppdi.com/

Mailing Address: Illoura Plaza, Suite 1, Level 4, 424 St. Kilda Road, Melbourne VIC 3004, Australia

Telephone 1: +61 3 9804 5211

Telephone 2: N/A

Fax: +61 3 9804 5233

Email: N/A

Country: **Australia**

StudyBuilder AU

EDC Products: StudyBuilder

Services:

EDC:	Yes
eDiary/ePRO:	Yes
IVRS:	N/A
Mobile Devices:	Yes

Web Site: www.studybuilder.com/au

Mailing Address: N/A

Telephone 1: +44 18 6533 8092

Telephone 2: 02 8011 3022

Fax: +44 18 6533 8100

Email: au@studybuilder.com

Country: **Australia**

Austria

Austrian Research Centers

EDC Products: Proprietory EDC system

Services:

EDC:	Yes
eDiary/ePRO:	N/A
IVRS:	N/A
Mobile Devices:	N/A

Web Site: http://www.arcsmed.at/

Mailing Address: DI Dr. Günter Schreier, MSc, Geschäftsfeldleiter,Reininghausstraße 13/1, 8020 Graz, Austria

Telephone 1: +43 (0)316 / 586 570-11

Telephone 2: N/A

Fax: N/A

Email: guenter.schreier@arcsmed.at

Country: **Austria**

Harrison Clinical Research Eastern Europe

EDC Products: Marvin

Services:

EDC:	Yes
eDiary/ePRO:	Yes
IVRS:	N/A
Mobile Devices:	N/A

Web Site: http://www.harrisonclinical.com

Mailing Address: Forschungsgesellschaft mbH, Parkring 10, 1010 Vienna, Austria

Telephone 1: 0043-1-516 33 3846

Telephone 2: N/A

Fax: 0043-1-516 33 3000

Email: N/A

Country: **Austria**

Premier Research

EDC Products: Oracle Clinical Remote Data Capture

Services:

EDC:	Yes
eDiary/ePRO:	N/A
IVRS:	N/A
Mobile Devices:	N/A

Web Site: http://www.premier-research.com

Mailing Address: Argentinierstrasse 26/5, A-1040 Wien, Austria

Telephone 1: +43 (0) 1/505 2628-0

Telephone 2: N/A

Fax: +43 (0) 1/505 2628-10

Email: N/A

Country: **Austria**

StudyBuilder AT

EDC Products: StudyBuilder

Services:

EDC:	Yes
eDiary/ePRO:	Yes
IVRS:	N/A
Mobile Devices:	Yes

Web Site: www.studybuilder.com/at

Mailing Address: Abteilung AA1146, Postfach 1000, 1150 WIEN, Austria

Telephone 1: +44 18 6533 8092

Telephone 2: N/A

Fax: +44 1865 338100

Email: at@studybuilder.com, info@studybuilder.at

EDC Providers

Country: **Austria**

Belgium

Country: **Belgium**

Adobe Systems Benelux BV

EDC Products: Adobe LiveCycle ES

Services:

EDC:	Yes
eDiary/ePRO:	N/A
IVRS:	N/A
Mobile Devices:	N/A

Web Site:
http://www.adobe.com/lifesciences/solutions/live cycle/

Mailing Address: Park Lane Building F, 1st floor, Culliganlaan 2F, B-1831 Diegem, Belgium

Telephone 1: +32 2416 4000

Telephone 2: N/A

Fax: +32 2416 4009

Email: Use website for communication

Country: **Belgium**

ClinSource NV

EDC Products: TrialXS

Services:

EDC:	Yes
eDiary/ePRO:	N/A
IVRS:	N/A
Mobile Devices:	N/A

Web Site: http://www.clinsource.com

Mailing Address: Mechelsesteenweg 455 Bus 2, B-1950 Kraainem (Brussels), Belgium

Telephone 1: + 32 2766 0080

Telephone 2: N/A

Fax: +32 2766 0081

Email: info@clinsource.com

Country: **Belgium**

eclinics Solutions

EDC Products: Not specified

Services:

EDC:	Yes
eDiary/ePRO:	Yes
IVRS:	N/A
Mobile Devices:	Yes

Web Site: http://www.eclinicssolutions.com

Mailing Address: Omega Business Park Wayenborgstraat 24, B 2800 Mechelen Belgium

Telephone 1: +32 1528 9030

Telephone 2: N/A

Fax: +32 1528 9031

Email: pvc@arco.be

Country: **Belgium**

Harrison Clinical Research SR

EDC Products: Marvin

Services:

EDC:	Yes
eDiary/ePRO:	Yes
IVRS:	N/A
Mobile Devices:	N/A

Web Site: http://www.harrisonclinical.com

Mailing Address: Leopold II Iaan 281, 1081 Brussel, Belgium

Telephone 1: +32 2469 3971

Telephone 2: N/A

Fax: +32 2465 5623

Email: N/A

Lambda-Plus

EDC Products: Electronic Data Management (EDM™)

Services:

EDC:	Yes
eDiary/ePRO:	N/A
IVRS:	N/A
Mobile Devices:	Yes

Web Site: http://www.lambdaplus.com

Mailing Address: Crealys Science Park, Business Center Vega, Rue Camille Hubert, 5, 5032, Gembloux, Belgium

Telephone 1: +32 8146 8046

Telephone 2: N/A

Fax: +32 8146 8047

Email: info@lambdaplus.com

Country: **Belgium**

Phase Forward Belgium

EDC Products: InForm™, Clintrial™, WebSDM™

Services:

EDC:	Yes
eDiary/ePRO:	N/A
IVRS:	N/A
Mobile Devices:	N/A

Web Site: http://www.phaseforward.com

Mailing Address: 155 Chaussée de Tervuren, Waterloo 1410, Belgium

Telephone 1: +32 2352 0830

Telephone 2: N/A

Fax: +32 2352 0839

Email: info.europe@phaseforward.com

Country: **Belgium**

PPD

EDC Products: Acceliant eClinical Suite, Oracle Clinical Remote Data Capture

Services:

EDC:	Yes
eDiary/ePRO:	N/A
IVRS:	Yes
Mobile Devices:	N/A

Web Site: http://www.ppdi.com/

Mailing Address: Romboutsstraat, 1, B-1932, St. Stevens Woluwe, Brussels, Belgium

Telephone 1: +32 2723 2626

Telephone 2: N/A

Fax: +32 2723 2600

Email: N/A

Country: **Belgium**

SGS Belgium NV

EDC Products: Phase Forward InForm

Services:

EDC:	Yes
eDiary/ePRO:	N/A
IVRS:	N/A
Mobile Devices:	N/A

Web Site: http://www.clinicalresearch.sgs.com

Mailing Address: Generaal de Wittelaan 19, A bus 5 2800 Mechelen, Belgium

Telephone 1: +32 1527 3245

Telephone 2: N/A

Fax: N/A

Email: N/A

Country: **Belgium**

StudyBuilder BE

EDC Products: StudyBuilder

Services:

EDC:	Yes
eDiary/ePRO:	Yes
IVRS:	N/A
Mobile Devices:	Yes

Web Site: http://www.studybuilder.com/

Mailing Address: Dept. AA1146, Postbus 71, 90/99 GENT X, Belgium

Telephone 1: +44 18 6533 8092

Telephone 2: N/A

Fax: +44 18 6533 8100

Email: be@studybuilder.com

Country: **Belgium**

Symfo

EDC Products: SymPRO, SymQOL, SymVoice, SymEDC, SymPhone

Services:

    EDC: Yes

    eDiary/ePRO: Yes

    IVRS: Yes

    Mobile Devices: Yes

Web Site: http://www.symfo.com/

Mailing Address: 239, Ave. Winston Churchill, B-1180, Brussels, Belgium

Telephone 1: +32 2340 8228

Telephone 2: N/A

Fax: N/A

Email: info@symfo.com

Country: **Belgium**

United Biosource Corporation

EDC Products: ClinPlus® Data Management System, SAS®-based

Services:

EDC:	Yes
eDiary/ePRO:	Yes
IVRS:	Yes
Mobile Devices:	Yes

Web Site: http://www.unitedbiosource.com

Mailing Address: Avenue A. Lacomble 69-71, 1030 Brussels, Belgium

Telephone 1: +32 2738 7862

Telephone 2: N/A

Fax: +32 2738 7866

Email: info@unitedbiosource.com

Country: **Belgium**

UNITHINK NV

EDC Products: UNITHINK EDC, UNITHINK eCRF

Services:

EDC: Yes

eDiary/ePRO: N/A

IVRS: N/A

Mobile Devices: N/A

Web Site: http://www.unithink.org/

Mailing Address: Waterfront Researchpark, Galileilaan 18, 2870 NIEL (Antwerp), Belgium

Telephone 1: +32 3298 0057

Telephone 2: N/A

Fax: +32 3298 0047

Email: info@unithink.org

EDC Providers

Country: **Belgium**

Brazil

Country: **Brazil**

Adobe Systems Brazil

EDC Products: Adobe LiveCycle ES

Services:

EDC:	Yes
eDiary/ePRO:	N/A
IVRS:	N/A
Mobile Devices:	N/A

Web Site:
http://www.adobe.com/lifesciences/solutions/live cycle/

Mailing Address: Rua Gomes de Carvalho, 1510 conjunto 121, Vila Olímpia, São Paulo, CEP 04547-005 SP, Brazil

Telephone 1: +55 11 2175 9595

Telephone 2: N/A

Fax: +55 11 3842 9539

Email: Use website for communication

ICON Clinical Research

EDC Products: Medidata Rave™

Services:

EDC:	Yes
eDiary/ePRO:	N/A
IVRS:	N/A
Mobile Devices:	N/A

Web Site: htpp://www.iconclinical.com/

Mailing Address: Avenida Ibirapuera, 2332 - Torre II - 4o andar, Moema, São Paulo, SP, CEP: 04028-003, Brazil

Telephone 1: +55 11 3525 5710

Telephone 2: N/A

Fax: +55 11 3525 5701

Email: info@iconaus.com.au

Country: **Brazil**

PPD

EDC Products: Acceliant eClinical Suite, Oracle Clinical Remote Data Capture

Services:

EDC:	Yes
eDiary/ePRO:	N/A
IVRS:	Yes
Mobile Devices:	N/A

Web Site: http://www.ppdi.com/

Mailing Address: Rua Leopoldo, Couto de Magalhães Jr., 758, 7 , 04542-000, São Paulo SP Brazil

Telephone 1: +55 11 4504 4700

Telephone 2: N/A

Fax: +55 11 4504 4849

Email: N/A

Bulgaria

Country: **Bulgaria**

Premier Research

<u>EDC Products:</u> Oracle Clinical Remote Data Capture

<u>Services:</u>

EDC:	Yes
eDiary/ePRO:	N/A
IVRS:	N/A
Mobile Devices:	N/A

<u>Web Site:</u> http://www.premier-research.com

<u>Mailing Address:</u> Expo 2000 Business Centre, 55 N. Vaptzarov Blvd., BG-1407 Sofia, Bulgaria

<u>Telephone 1:</u> +359 2933 1740

<u>Telephone 2:</u> N/A

<u>Fax:</u> +359 2933 1743

<u>Email:</u> N/A

Canada

Country: **Canada**

Adobe Systems Canada

EDC Products: Adobe LiveCycle ES

Services:

EDC:	Yes
eDiary/ePRO:	N/A
IVRS:	N/A
Mobile Devices:	N/A

Web Site:
http://www.adobe.com/lifesciences/solutions/live cycle/

Mailing Address: 3250 Bloor Street West, Suite 1200, Etobicoke, Ontario M8X 2X9, Canada

Telephone 1: +1 647 288 6400

Telephone 2: N/A

Fax: +1 647 288 6429

Email: Use website for communication

Axiom Real-time Metrics

EDC Products: Axiom Go3 Clinical Trial Workflow & Management Suite

Services:

EDC:	Yes
eDiary/ePRO:	N/A
IVRS:	N/A
Mobile Devices:	N/A

Web Site: http://www.axiommetrics.com/

Mailing Address: 8-1400 Cornwall Road, Oakville, Ontario, Canada, L6J 7W5

Telephone 1: +1 905 845 9779

Telephone 2: N/A

Fax: +1 905 849 3146

Email: info@axiommetrics.com

Country: **Canada**

Cardinal systems

EDC Products: InfoGate

Services:

EDC:	Yes
eDiary/ePRO:	N/A
IVRS:	Yes
Mobile Devices:	N/A

Web Site: http://www.cardinal-sys.com/

Mailing Address: 5532, Kaye Street, Halifax, Canada

Telephone 1: +33 1 5336 2462

Telephone 2: +1 902 448 5431

Fax: N/A

Email: contact@cardinal-sys.com

Clinical DataFax Systems Inc.

EDC Products: DataFax, iDataFax

Services:

EDC: Yes

eDiary/ePRO: N/A

IVRS: N/A

Mobile Devices: N/A

Web Site: http://www.datafax.com

Mailing Address: 25 Main Street West, Suite 500, Hamilton, Ontario, Canada L8P 1H1

Telephone 1: +1 905 522 3282

Telephone 2: N/A

Fax: +1 905 522 7284

Email: info@datafax.com

Clinimetrics

<u>EDC Products:</u> Oracle™ Clinical Remote Data Capture (RDC)

<u>Services:</u>

      EDC: Yes

      eDiary/ePRO: N/A

      IVRS: N/A

      Mobile Devices: N/A

<u>Web Site:</u> http://www.clinimetrics.com

<u>Mailing Address:</u> 2655 North Sheridan Way, Suite 120, Mississauga, Ontario, L5K 2P8, Canada

<u>Telephone 1:</u> +1 905 403 9901

<u>Telephone 2:</u> N/A

<u>Fax:</u> +1 905 403 9083

<u>Email:</u> N/A

Echidna Solutions Corporation

<u>EDC Products:</u> custom built EDC software

<u>Services:</u>

    EDC: Yes

    eDiary/ePRO: N/A

    IVRS: N/A

    Mobile Devices: N/A

<u>Web Site:</u> http://www.echidna.ca

<u>Mailing Address:</u> 207 King St., London, Ontario N6A 1C9, Canada

<u>Telephone 1:</u> +1 519 858 9604

<u>Telephone 2:</u> +1 877 858 9604

<u>Fax:</u> N/A

<u>Email:</u> contact@echidna.ca

Country: **Canada**

eclinics Solutions

EDC Products: Not specified

Services:

EDC:	Yes
eDiary/ePRO:	Yes
IVRS:	N/A
Mobile Devices:	Yes

Web Site: http://www.eclinicssolutions.com

Mailing Address: 50, St-Charles W. Suite 304 Longueuil, Québec, Canada J4H 1C6

Telephone 1: +1 450 646 4606

Telephone 2: N/A

Fax: +1 450 646 4303

Email: pgalame@eclinicssolutions.com

Country: **Canada**

i3 Statprobe

EDC Products: Oracle® Clinical Remote Data Capture (OC RDC)

Services:

EDC:	Yes
eDiary/ePRO:	N/A
IVRS:	N/A
Mobile Devices:	N/A

Web Site:
http://www.i3global.com/Businesses/i3Statprobe
/

Mailing Address: Burlington, Ontario, Canada

Telephone 1: +1 866 427 6848

Telephone 2: +1 801 982 3402

Fax: N/A

Email: N/A

Country: **Canada**

ICON Clinical Research

EDC Products: Medidata Rave™

Services:

EDC:	Yes
eDiary/ePRO:	N/A
IVRS:	N/A
Mobile Devices:	N/A

Web Site: htpp://www.iconclinical.com/

Mailing Address: 7405 Transcanada Highway, Suite 300, Montreal H4T 1Z2, Canada

Telephone 1: +1 514 332 0700

Telephone 2: N/A

Fax: +1 514 332 0710

Email: info@iconcan.com

Country: **Canada**

Integrated Research Inc.

EDC Products: eData ManagementTM by eResearch TechnologyTM

Services:

EDC:	Yes
eDiary/ePRO:	N/A
IVRS:	N/A
Mobile Devices:	N/A

Web Site: http://www.iricanada.ca

Mailing Address: 1351 Sunnybrooke Boulevard, Dollard-des-Ormeaux (Montreal), Quebec, Canada H9B 3K9

Telephone 1: +1 800 780 9135

Telephone 2: +1 514 683 1909

Fax: +1 514 683 0121

Email: info@iricanada.com

McKesson Phase 4 Solutions

EDC Products: not specified

Services:

EDC:	Yes
eDiary/ePRO:	N/A
IVRS:	Yes
Mobile Devices:	N/A

Web Site: http://www.mckesson.ca

Mailing Address: 1 Concorde Gate, 4th Floor, Toronto Ontario, M3C 3N6, Canada

Telephone 1: +1 416 429 6172

Telephone 2: +1 800 811 9880

Fax: +1 416 429 2745

Email: communications@mckesson.ca

Country: **Canada**

Palm Inc.

EDC Products: Diet & Exercise Assistant. Taber's Cyclopedic Medical Dictionary. Nursing Central. Davis's Drug Guide. Palm Diabetic Diary. 5 Minute Clinical Consult. HeathFile Plus. CalorieKing Handheld Diet Diary. Biometric Weight Manager. ER Suite.

Services:

EDC:	N/A
eDiary/ePRO:	Yes
IVRS:	N/A
Mobile Devices:	Yes

Web Site:
http://www.palm.com/us/software/health.html

Mailing Address: 2680 Skymark Avenue, Suite 410, P.O. Box 9, Mississauga, Ontario, L4W 5L6, Canada

Telephone 1: +1 800 881 7256

Telephone 2: +1 877 597 7256

Fax: N/A

Email: volumepurchases@store.palm.com

Country: **Canada**

PPD

EDC Products: Acceliant eClinical Suite, Oracle Clinical Remote Data Capture

Services:

EDC:	Yes
eDiary/ePRO:	N/A
IVRS:	Yes
Mobile Devices:	N/A

Web Site: http://www.ppdi.com/

Mailing Address: 2700 Matheson Blvd. East, East Tower, Ste. 300, Mississauga, Ontario, Canada, L4W 4V9

Telephone 1: +1 905 625 3400

Telephone 2: N/A

Fax: +1 905 625 0814

Email: N/A

Country: **Canada**

SciAn Services

EDC Products: EDCpro

Services:

EDC:	Yes
eDiary/ePRO:	N/A
IVRS:	N/A
Mobile Devices:	N/A

Web Site: http://www.scian.com/;
http://www.edcpro.com/index.html

Mailing Address: 4174 Dundas Street West, Suite 300, Toronto, ON M8X 1X3, Canada

Telephone 1: +1 416 231 8008

Telephone 2: N/A

Fax: +1 416 231 1422

Email: BusinessDevelopment@scian.com

Country: **Canada**

StudyBuilder Limited

EDC Products: StudyBuilder

Services:

EDC:	Yes
eDiary/ePRO:	Yes
IVRS:	N/A
Mobile Devices:	Yes

Web Site: www.studybuilder.com/ca

Mailing Address: N/A

Telephone 1: +44 18 6533 8092

Telephone 2: N/A

Fax: +44 18 6533 8100

Email: ca@studybuilder.com

Stylus Metrics

EDC Products: The Academic Medical Mobile Record System (AM-MRS)

Services:

EDC:	N/A
eDiary/ePRO:	Yes
IVRS:	N/A
Mobile Devices:	Yes

Web Site: http://www.stylusmetrics.com/

Mailing Address: Suite #206, 4616 - Valiant Drive N.W., Calgary, Alberta, Canada T3A 0X9

Telephone 1: +1 403 208 3223

Telephone 2: N/A

Fax: +1 403 208 5031

Email: Information@StylusMetrics.com

Country: **Canada**

SyMetric Sciences, Inc.

EDC Products: «SyMetric»™, Mesh

Services:

EDC:	Yes
eDiary/ePRO:	Yes
IVRS:	N/A
Mobile Devices:	N/A

Web Site: http://www.symetric.ca/

Mailing Address: 1-2082 Sherbrooke West, Montreal, Quebec, Canada, H3H 1G5

Telephone 1: +1 514 935 4562

Telephone 2: N/A

Fax: +1 514 935 9911

Email: major@symetric.ca

Country: **Canada**

Syreon Corporation

EDC Products: ClinStream

Services:

EDC:	Yes
eDiary/ePRO:	N/A
IVRS:	N/A
Mobile Devices:	N/A

Web Site: www.syreon.com

Mailing Address: 450 - 1385 West 8th Avenue, Vancouver, BC V6H 3V9, Canada

Telephone 1: +1 604 676 5900

Telephone 2: N/A

Fax: +1 604 676 5911

Email: info@syreon.com

TrialStat Corporation

EDC Products: ClinicalAnalytics

Services:

        EDC: Yes

        eDiary/ePRO: N/A

        IVRS: N/A

        Mobile Devices: N/A

Web Site: http://www.trialstat.com

Mailing Address: 1101 Prince of Wales Drive, Suite 200, Ottawa, Ontario, Canada K2C 3W7

Telephone 1:   +1 613 741 9909

Telephone 2:   +1 866 416 STAT

Fax: +1 613 274 3674

Email: info@trialstat.com

United Biosource Corporation

EDC Products: ClinPlus® Data Management System, SAS®-based

Services:

EDC:	Yes
eDiary/ePRO:	Yes
IVRS:	Yes
Mobile Devices:	Yes

Web Site: http://www.unitedbiosource.com

Mailing Address: 185 Dorval Avenue, Suite 500, Montreal, Quebec H9S 5J9, Canada

Telephone 1: +1 514 422 8271

Telephone 2: N/A

Fax: +1 514 422 8272

Email: info@unitedbiosource.com

Chile

ICON Clinical Research

EDC Products: Medidata Rave™

Services:

EDC:	Yes
eDiary/ePRO:	N/A
IVRS:	N/A
Mobile Devices:	N/A

Web Site: htpp://www.iconclinical.com/

Mailing Address: Edificio Milenium, Av. Vitacura 2939, Piso 10, Las Condes, 7550011 Santiago, Chile

Telephone 1: +56 2431 5093

Telephone 2: N/A

Fax: N/A

Email: N/A

EDC Providers

Country: **Chile**

PPD

EDC Products: Acceliant eClinical Suite, Oracle Clinical Remote Data Capture

Services:

EDC:	Yes
eDiary/ePRO:	N/A
IVRS:	Yes
Mobile Devices:	N/A

Web Site: http://www.ppdi.com/

Mailing Address: Vitacura 2939, Piso 19, Oficina 1902, Edificio Millenium, Las Condes, Santiago, Chile

Telephone 1: +56 2460 6600

Telephone 2: N/A

Fax: +56 2435 0036

Email: N/A

EDC Providers

Country: **Chile**

China

Country: **China**

Adobe Systems Incorporated

EDC Products: Adobe LiveCycle ES

Services:

EDC:	Yes
eDiary/ePRO:	N/A
IVRS:	N/A
Mobile Devices:	N/A

Web Site:
http://www.adobe.com/lifesciences/solutions/live cycle/

Mailing Address: Room 309, West Wing, China World Trade Center, No.1 Jian Wai Da Jie, Beijing 100004, P.R. China

Telephone 1: +86 10 5865 7700

Telephone 2: N/A

Fax: +86 10 5865 7701

Email: Use website for communication

ICON Clinical Research

EDC Products: Medidata Rave™

Services:

EDC:	Yes
eDiary/ePRO:	N/A
IVRS:	N/A
Mobile Devices:	N/A

Web Site: htpp://www.iconclinical.com/

Mailing Address: Suite 1008, North Building, Junefield Plaza, No. 6 Xuanwumenwai Ave, Beijing P.R China 100052

Telephone 1: +86 10 6310 6300

Telephone 2: N/A

Fax: +86 10 6310 7446

Email: info@iconaus.com.au

PPD

<u>**EDC Products:**</u> Acceliant eClinical Suite, Oracle Clinical Remote Data Capture

<u>**Services:**</u>

EDC:	Yes
eDiary/ePRO:	N/A
IVRS:	Yes
Mobile Devices:	N/A

<u>**Web Site:**</u>   http://www.ppdi.com/

<u>**Mailing Address:**</u> Unit 815, Beijing New World Centre, South Office Tower, No. 3A Chongwenmenwai Da Jie, Chongwen District, Beijing 100062, China

<u>**Telephone 1:**</u>   +86 10 6709 2270

<u>**Telephone 2:**</u>   N/A

<u>**Fax:**</u>   +86 10 6709 2370

<u>**Email:**</u>   N/A

Country: **China**

StudyBuilder Limited

EDC Products: StudyBuilder

Services:

EDC:	Yes
eDiary/ePRO:	Yes
IVRS:	N/A
Mobile Devices:	Yes

Web Site: http://www.studybuilder.com/

Mailing Address: N/A

Telephone 1: +44 18 6533 8092

Telephone 2: +85 2 8171 3304

Fax: +44 18 6533 8100

Email: cn@studybuilder.com

Croatia

Country: **Croatia**

Utilis Ltd.

EDC Products: .CRF

Services:

EDC:	Yes
eDiary/ePRO:	N/A
IVRS:	N/A
Mobile Devices:	N/A

Web Site: http://www.utilis.biz/

Mailing Address: Technology Park, Dragutina Golika 63, 10000 Zagreb, Croatia

Telephone 1: +385 1363 5666

Telephone 2: N/A

Fax: +385 1363 0469

Email: info@utilis.biz

Czech Republic

Country: **Czech Republic**

Chiltern International Limited

EDC Products: Not specified

Services:

        EDC: Yes

        eDiary/ePRO: N/A

        IVRS: N/A

        Mobile Devices: N/A

Web Site: http://www2.chiltern.com/

Mailing Address: Budova A2, Pod Visnovkou, 31/1661, 140 00 Praha, 4-Krc, Czech Republic

Telephone 1:   +420 234 708 911

Telephone 2:   +420 234 708 912

Fax: +420 234 708 913

Email: N/A

Country: **Czech Republic**

ICON Clinical Research

<u>**EDC Products:**</u> Medidata Rave™

<u>**Services:**</u>

EDC: Yes

eDiary/ePRO: N/A

IVRS: N/A

Mobile Devices: N/A

<u>**Web Site:**</u> htpp://www.iconclinical.com/

<u>**Mailing Address:**</u> V parku 2335/20, Chodov, 148 00 Praha 4, IC O: 28171586, Czech Republic

<u>**Telephone 1:**</u> +420 272 124 000

<u>**Telephone 2:**</u> N/A

<u>**Fax:**</u> +420 272 124 097

<u>**Email:**</u> N/A

Country: **Czech Republic**

PPD

EDC Products: Acceliant eClinical Suite, Oracle Clinical Remote Data Capture

Services:

EDC:	Yes
eDiary/ePRO:	N/A
IVRS:	Yes
Mobile Devices:	N/A

Web Site: http://www.ppdi.com/

Mailing Address: Budejovicka alej, Antala Staska 2027/79, 140 00 Praha 4, Czech Republic

Telephone 1: +420 233 321 233

Telephone 2: N/A

Fax: +420 233 323 457

Email: N/A

Country: **Czech Republic**

Premier Research

<u>EDC Products:</u> Oracle Clinical Remote Data Capture

<u>Services:</u>

EDC:	Yes
eDiary/ePRO:	N/A
IVRS:	N/A
Mobile Devices:	N/A

<u>Web Site:</u>   http://www.premier-research.com

<u>Mailing Address:</u> Xaveriova s.r.o, CZ - 15000 Praha 5, Czech Republic

<u>Telephone 1:</u>   +420 251 101 201

<u>Telephone 2:</u>   N/A

<u>Fax:</u>   +420 251 101 202

<u>Email:</u>   N/A

Country: **Czech Republic**

United Biosource Corporation

<u>**EDC Products:**</u> ClinPlus® Data Management System, SAS®-based

<u>**Services:**</u>

       EDC: Yes

       eDiary/ePRO: Yes

       IVRS: Yes

       Mobile Devices: Yes

<u>**Web Site:**</u>   http://www.unitedbiosource.com

<u>**Mailing Address:**</u> Meteor Office Center, Sokolovska 100/94, 186 00 Praha 8, Czech Republic

<u>**Telephone 1:**</u>   +420 236-080-100

<u>**Telephone 2:**</u>   N/A

<u>**Fax:**</u>   +420 236 080 105

<u>**Email:**</u>   training@unitedbiosource.com

Denmark

Country: **Denmark**

aCROnordic A/S

EDC Products: Oracle Clinical

Services:

EDC:	Yes
eDiary/ePRO:	N/A
IVRS:	N/A
Mobile Devices:	N/A

Web Site: htpp://www.acronordic.com/

Mailing Address: Scion DTU, Kogle Allé 5, DK-2970 Hørsholm, Denmark

Telephone 1: +45 4516 8800

Telephone 2: N/A

Fax: +45 4516 8801

Email: info@aCROnordic.com

Adobe Systems Danmark A/S

<u>EDC Products:</u> Adobe LiveCycle ES

<u>Services:</u>

EDC:	Yes
eDiary/ePRO:	N/A
IVRS:	N/A
Mobile Devices:	N/A

<u>Web Site:</u>
http://www.adobe.com/lifesciences/solutions/live cycle/

<u>Mailing Address:</u> Gydevang   39-41,   3450   Allerød, København, Danmark

<u>Telephone 1:</u>   +45 4813 1313

<u>Telephone 2:</u>   N/A

<u>Fax:</u>   +45 4813 1312

<u>Email:</u>   Use   website   for   communication

Country: **Denmark**

ICON Clinical Research

EDC Products: Medidata Rave™

Services:

EDC:	Yes
eDiary/ePRO:	N/A
IVRS:	N/A
Mobile Devices:	N/A

Web Site: htpp://www.iconclinical.com/

Mailing Address: Tuborg Boulevard 12,3, 2900 Hellerup, Denmark

Telephone 1: +45 7020 4015

Telephone 2: N/A

Fax: N/A

Email: N/A

Country: **Denmark**

PPD

EDC Products: Acceliant eClinical Suite, Oracle Clinical Remote Data Capture

Services:

EDC:	Yes
eDiary/ePRO:	N/A
IVRS:	Yes
Mobile Devices:	N/A

Web Site: http://www.ppdi.com/

Mailing Address: Regus South Harbour, Sluseholmen 2-4, 2450 Copenhagen SV, Denmark

Telephone 1: +45 3694 4556

Telephone 2: N/A

Fax: +45 3694 4770

Email: N/A

Country: **Denmark**

StudyBuilder DK

EDC Products: StudyBuilder

Services:

EDC:	Yes
eDiary/ePRO:	Yes
IVRS:	N/A
Mobile Devices:	Yes

Web Site: http://www.studybuilder.com/

Mailing Address: Dept. AA1146, Box 0553, 1532 København V, Denmark

Telephone 1: +44 18 6533 8092

Telephone 2: N/A

Fax: +44 18 6533 8100

Email: dk@studybuilder.com

Finland

CRF Inc.

EDC Products: TrialMax®

Services:

EDC:	N/A
eDiary/ePRO:	Yes
IVRS:	N/A
Mobile Devices:	Yes

Web Site: http://www.crfhealth.com/

Mailing Address: Simonkatu   8A,   FI-00100   Helsinki, Finland

Telephone 1:   +358 201 700 700

Telephone 2:   N/A

Fax: +358 201 700 710

Email: info-finland@crfhealth.com

Country: **Finland**

ICON Clinical Research

EDC Products: Medidata Rave™

Services:

EDC:	Yes
eDiary/ePRO:	N/A
IVRS:	N/A
Mobile Devices:	N/A

Web Site: htpp://www.iconclinical.com/

Mailing Address: Mannerheimintie 12B, 5th Floor, 00100 Helsinki, Finland

Telephone 1: +358 925 166 221

Telephone 2: N/A

Fax: N/A

Email: N/A

Country: **Finland**

StudyBuilder FI

EDC Products: StudyBuilder

Services:

EDC:	Yes
eDiary/ePRO:	Yes
IVRS:	N/A
Mobile Devices:	Yes

Web Site: http://www.studybuilder.com/

Mailing Address: Sopimus 00003-013, 00002 Helsinki, Finland

Telephone 1: +44 18 6533 8092

Telephone 2: N/A

Fax: +44 18 6533 8100

Email: fi@studybuilder.com

EDC Providers

Country: **France**

France

Country: **France**

Adobe Systems France SAS

EDC Products: Adobe LiveCycle ES

Services:

EDC:	Yes
eDiary/ePRO:	N/A
IVRS:	N/A
Mobile Devices:	N/A

Web Site:
http://www.adobe.com/lifesciences/solutions/live cycle/

Mailing Address: 112, avenue Kléber, 75784 Paris Cedex 16, France

Telephone 1: +33 1 5654 9900

Telephone 2: N/A

Fax: +33 1 5654 9901

Email: Use website for communication

Arone

EDC Products: DMRunner

Services:

EDC:	Yes
eDiary/ePRO:	N/A
IVRS:	N/A
Mobile Devices:	N/A

Web Site: http://www.arone.com/

Mailing Address: 23, rue du Commandant Jean Duhail, 94120 FONTENAY SOUS BOIS, France

Telephone 1: +33 1 4876 8916

Telephone 2: +33 1 4883 6929

Fax: +33 1 5597 1314

Email: info-arone@arone.com

Country: **France**

Ascopharm

<u>**EDC Products:**</u> Projection™

<u>**Services:**</u>

       EDC: Yes

       eDiary/ePRO: N/A

       IVRS: N/A

       Mobile Devices: N/A

<u>**Web Site:**</u>   http://www.ascopharm.com

<u>**Mailing Address:**</u> 16-18 rue de Londres, 75009 Paris, France

<u>**Telephone 1:**</u>   +33 1 5633 3540

<u>**Telephone 2:**</u>   N/A

<u>**Fax:**</u>   +33 1 5633 3550

<u>**Email:**</u>   ascopharm@ascopharm.com

Country: **France**

Cardinal systems

EDC Products: InfoGate

Services:

EDC:	Yes
eDiary/ePRO:	N/A
IVRS:	Yes
Mobile Devices:	N/A

Web Site: http://www.cardinal-sys.com/

Mailing Address: 91, avenue de la République, 75011 Paris, France

Telephone 1: +33 1 4021 1900

Telephone 2: N/A

Fax: +33 1 4021 9495

Email: contact@cardinal-sys.com

Country: **France**

Chiltern International Limited

EDC Products: Not specified

Services:

    EDC: Yes

    eDiary/ePRO: N/A

    IVRS: N/A

    Mobile Devices: N/A

Web Site: http://www2.chiltern.com/

Mailing Address: Immeuble Le Toronto - 2eme etage, 54 Route de Sartrouville, 78232 - Le Pecq, France

Telephone 1: +33 1 3480 3050

Telephone 2: N/A

Fax: +33 1 3480 3060

Email: N/A

EDC Providers

Country: **France**

ClinPhone Group Ltd.

<u>EDC Products:</u> Combined EDC-IVR: DataLabs by ClinPhone (EDC/CDMS) and ClinPhone IVR/IWR

<u>Services:</u>

EDC: Yes

eDiary/ePRO: Yes

IVRS: Yes

Mobile Devices: N/A

<u>Web Site:</u> http://www.clinphone.com

<u>Mailing Address:</u> Tour de l'horloge, 4 Place Louis Armand, 75603 Paris Cedex 12, France

<u>Telephone 1:</u> +33 1 4397 1401

<u>Telephone 2:</u> N/A

<u>Fax:</u> +33 1 7276 8024

<u>Email:</u> info@clinphone.com

Country: **France**

CONSIGNIA FRANCE

EDC Products: StudyBuilder

Services:

EDC:	Yes
eDiary/ePRO:	Yes
IVRS:	N/A
Mobile Devices:	Yes

Web Site: www.studybuilder.com/fr

Mailing Address: Dept. AA1146, 92609 ASNIERES SUR SEINE, CEDEX, France

Telephone 1: +44 18 6533 8092

Telephone 2: N/A

Fax: +44 18 6533 8100

Email: fr@studybuilder.com

Harrison Clinical Research France

EDC Products: Marvin

Services:

EDC:	Yes
eDiary/ePRO:	Yes
IVRS:	N/A
Mobile Devices:	N/A

Web Site: http://www.harrisonclinical.com

Mailing Address: 3 rue Bellanger, 92300 Levallois-Perret, France

Telephone 1: +33 1 5590 5710

Telephone 2: N/A

Fax: +33 1 5590 1038

Email: N/A

ICON Clinical Research

EDC Products: Medidata Rave™

Services:

EDC:	Yes
eDiary/ePRO:	N/A
IVRS:	N/A
Mobile Devices:	N/A

Web Site: htpp://www.iconclinical.com/

Mailing Address: 20 Rue Troyon, 92310 Sevres, Paris, France

Telephone 1: +33 1 4629 6500

Telephone 2: N/A

Fax: +33 1 4629 6501

Email: N/A

Country: **France**

KIKA SA

EDC Products: Eventa™

Services:

EDC:	Yes
eDiary/ePRO:	N/A
IVRS:	N/A
Mobile Devices:	N/A

Web Site: http://www.kikamedical.com/

Mailing Address: 35, rue de Rambouillet, 75012 Paris, France

Telephone 1: +33 1 5317 9570

Telephone 2: N/A

Fax: +33 1 4473 4011

Email: sales-eu@kikamedical.com

Country: **France**

Phase Forward SA

EDC Products: InForm™, Clintrial™, WebSDM™

Services:

        EDC: Yes

        eDiary/ePRO: N/A

        IVRS: N/A

        Mobile Devices: N/A

Web Site: http://www.phaseforward.com

Mailing Address: 1 bis rue du Petit-Clamart, BP71, 78143 Velizy Cedex, France

Telephone 1:   +33 1 4083 0707

Telephone 2:   N/A

Fax: +33 1 4083 0052

Email: info.europe@phaseforward.com

PPD

EDC Products: Acceliant eClinical Suite, Oracle Clinical
Remote Data Capture

Services:

EDC:	Yes
eDiary/ePRO:	N/A
IVRS:	Yes
Mobile Devices:	N/A

Web Site: http://www.ppdi.com/

Mailing Address: 45-47 Blvd. Paul Vaillant Couturier, 94853 Ivry-sur-Seine Cedex, France

Telephone 1: +33 1 5846 5846

Telephone 2: N/A

Fax: +33 1 5846 5870

Email: N/A

Country: **France**

Premier Research

<u>EDC Products:</u> Oracle Clinical Remote Data Capture

<u>Services:</u>

EDC:	Yes
eDiary/ePRO:	N/A
IVRS:	N/A
Mobile Devices:	N/A

<u>Web Site:</u>   http://www.premier-research.com

<u>Mailing Address:</u> 28 Bld Haussmann, 75009, Paris, France

<u>Telephone 1:</u>   +33 1 4450 1077

<u>Telephone 2:</u>   N/A

<u>Fax:</u>   +33 1 4015 0198

<u>Email:</u>   N/A

Country: **France**

SGS aster sas

EDC Products: Phase Forward InForm

Services:

EDC:	Yes
eDiary/ePRO:	N/A
IVRS:	N/A
Mobile Devices:	N/A

Web Site: http://www.clinicalresearch.sgs.com

Mailing Address: Clinical Research Unit, 3-5 rue Eugene Millon, 75015 Paris, France

Telephone 1: +33 1 5368 0868

Telephone 2: N/A

Fax: N/A

Email: N/A

Country: **France**

XClinical France

EDC Products: MARVIN

Services:

EDC:	Yes
eDiary/ePRO:	N/A
IVRS:	N/A
Mobile Devices:	N/A

Web Site: http://www.xclinical.com

Mailing Address: 86, Rue du Cherche-Midi, 75006 Paris, France

Telephone 1: +33 1 4544 1425

Telephone 2: N/A

Fax: +33 1 4544 1425

Email: info@xclinical.com

Germany

EDC Providers

Country: **Germany**

AAIPharma Inc.

<u>**EDC Products:**</u> multiple EDC platforms

<u>**Services:**</u>

        EDC: Yes

        eDiary/ePRO: N/A

        IVRS: N/A

        Mobile Devices: N/A

<u>**Web Site:**</u>   http://www.aaipharma.com/

<u>**Mailing Address:**</u> Wegenerstrasse 13, 89231 Neu-Ulm, Germany

<u>**Telephone 1:**</u> +49.731.9840.0

<u>**Telephone 2:**</u> N/A

<u>**Fax:**</u>   N/A

<u>**Email:**</u>   services@aaipharma.com

Country: **Germany**

Accovion GmbH

EDC Products: Oracle Clinical, Clintrial

Services:

EDC:	Yes
eDiary/ePRO:	Yes
IVRS:	N/A
Mobile Devices:	N/A

Web Site: http://www.accovion.com/

Mailing Address: Helfmann-Park 10, D - 65760 Eschborn (Frankfurt), Germany

Telephone 1:   +49 (6196) 77 09 - 0

Telephone 2:   N/A

Fax: +49 (6196) 77 09 - 120

Email: info@accovion.com

Adapt-EDC

EDC Products: ADAPT~EDC

Services:

    EDC: Yes

    eDiary/ePRO: N/A

    IVRS: N/A

    Mobile Devices: N/A

Web Site: http://www.adaptedc.com/

Mailing Address: Mühlgasse 9, D-88634 Herdwangen-Schönach, Germany

Telephone 1:   +49 - 7557 91015

Telephone 2:   N/A

Fax: N/A

Email: dshepherd@adaptedc.de

Country: **Germany**

Adobe Systems GmbH

EDC Products: Adobe LiveCycle ES

Services:

EDC:	Yes
eDiary/ePRO:	N/A
IVRS:	N/A
Mobile Devices:	N/A

Web Site:
http://www.adobe.com/lifesciences/solutions/livecycle/

Mailing Address: Georg-Brauchle-Ring 58, D-80992 München, Deutschland

Telephone 1: +49 89 31 70 50

Telephone 2: N/A

Fax: +49 89 31 70 57 05

Email: Use website for communication

Country: **Germany**

AMEDON GmbH

EDC Products: Amdeon eCRF

Services:

EDC:	Yes
eDiary/ePRO:	N/A
IVRS:	N/A
Mobile Devices:	N/A

Web Site: http://www.amedon.de/english

Mailing Address: Willy-Brandt-Allee 31c, 23554 Lübeck, Germany

Telephone 1: +49 (0) 451 / 38 450-0

Telephone 2: N/A

Fax: +49 (0) 451 / 38 450-11

Email: info@amedon.de

Country: **Germany**

Chiltern International Limited

EDC Products: Not specified

Services:

EDC: Yes

eDiary/ePRO: N/A

IVRS: N/A

Mobile Devices: N/A

Web Site: http://www2.chiltern.com/

Mailing Address: Norsk-Data-Strasse 1, D, 61352 Bad Homburg, Germany

Telephone 1:   + 49 (0) 6172 9443 0

Telephone 2:   N/A

Fax: + 49 (0) 6172 9443 300

Email: N/A

Country: **Germany**

clinIT AG

EDC Products: TRI@L-IT

Services:

EDC:	Yes
eDiary/ePRO:	N/A
IVRS:	N/A
Mobile Devices:	N/A

Web Site: http://www.clinit.net/

Mailing Address: Hornusstr. 16, 79108 Freiburg, Germany

Telephone 1: +49 761 50318 77

Telephone 2: N/A

Fax: +49 761 50318 30

Email: info@clinIT.net

ClinResearch GmbH

EDC Products: Oracle-based data management system

Services:

EDC: Yes

eDiary/ePRO: N/A

IVRS: N/A

Mobile Devices: N/A

Web Site: http://www.clinresearch.com/

Mailing Address: Robert-Perthel-Str. 77a, D-50739 Cologne, Germany

Telephone 1: +49 221 59990

Telephone 2: N/A

Fax: +49 221 5999400

Email: N/A

Country: **Germany**

DATATRAK Deutschland, GmbH

EDC Products: eClinical

Services:

EDC:	Yes
eDiary/ePRO:	Yes
IVRS:	Yes
Mobile Devices:	N/A

Web Site: http://www.datatrak.net

Mailing Address: Rochusstrasse 65, 53123 Bonn, Germany

Telephone 1: +49.228.979.8320

Telephone 2: N/A

Fax: +49.228.979.8334

Email: company@datatrak.net

Country: **Germany**

Dr. Oestreich + Partner GmbH

EDC Products: OPVerdi, PMSBOX

Services:

EDC:	Yes
eDiary/ePRO:	N/A
IVRS:	N/A
Mobile Devices:	Yes

Web Site: http://www.oandp-cro.com/

Mailing Address: Hansaring 102-104, D-50670 Cologne, Germany

Telephone 1: +49-(0)221-9128710

Telephone 2: N/A

Fax: +49-(0)221-9128711

Email: info@OandP-CRO.com

Country: **Germany**

Entimo AG

EDC Products: entimICE

Services:

EDC:	Yes
eDiary/ePRO:	Yes
IVRS:	N/A
Mobile Devices:	N/A

Web Site: http://www.entimo.com/

Mailing Address: Stralauer Platz 33-34, 10243 Berlin, Germany

Telephone 1: +49(0)30 520 024 100

Telephone 2: N/A

Fax: +49(0)30 520 024 101

Email: info@entimo.com

Country: **Germany**

Harrison Clinical Research Deutschland GmbH

EDC Products: Marvin

Services:

EDC: Yes

eDiary/ePRO: Yes

IVRS: N/A

Mobile Devices: N/A

Web Site: http://www.harrisonclinical.com

Mailing Address: Albrechtstrasse 14, 80636 Munich, Germany

Telephone 1: 49-(0)89-12 66 80-0

Telephone 2: N/A

Fax: 49-(0)89-12 66 80-2444

Email: N/A

Country: **Germany**

ICON Clinical Research

EDC Products: Medidata Rave™

Services:

 EDC: Yes

 eDiary/ePRO: N/A

 IVRS: N/A

 Mobile Devices: N/A

Web Site: htpp://www.iconclinical.com/

Mailing Address: Heinrich-Hertz-Strasse 26, D-63225, Langen, Germany

Telephone 1: +49 (6103) 9040

Telephone 2: N/A

Fax: +49 (6103) 904100

Email: N/A

Country: **Germany**

OmniComm Europe GmbH

EDC Products: TrialMaster®

Services:

EDC:	Yes
eDiary/ePRO:	N/A
IVRS:	N/A
Mobile Devices:	N/A

Web Site: http://www.omnicomm.com

Mailing Address: Bundeskanzlerplatz 2-10, Bonn 53113, Germany

Telephone 1: N/A

Telephone 2: N/A

Fax: N/A

Email: infoeurope@omnicomm.com

Country: **Germany**

Penguin Trials Ltd.

EDC Products: PhOSCo™

Services:

      EDC: Yes

      eDiary/ePRO: N/A

      IVRS: N/A

      Mobile Devices: N/A

Web Site: htpp://www.penguintrials.com/

Mailing Address: Postfach 3204, 40748 Langenfeld, Germany

Telephone 1: +49(0)2173/2692267

Telephone 2: N/A

Fax: +49(0)2173/2692268

Email: info@penguintrials.com

Country: **Germany**

Perceptive Informatics, Inc.

<u>EDC Products:</u> Perceptive Voice™, ALADDIN™, ePRO

<u>Services:</u>

EDC: N/A

eDiary/ePRO: Yes

IVRS: Yes

Mobile Devices: N/A

<u>Web Site:</u>   http://www.perceptive.com/

<u>Mailing Address:</u> Am Bahnhof Westend 11, 14059 Berlin, Germany

<u>Telephone 1:</u>   +49.30.30.685.5075

<u>Telephone 2:</u>   N/A

<u>Fax:</u>   +49.30.30.685.755

<u>Email:</u>   info@perceptive.com

Country: **Germany**

PPD

EDC Products: Acceliant eClinical Suite, Oracle Clinical Remote Data Capture

Services:

EDC:	Yes
eDiary/ePRO:	N/A
IVRS:	Yes
Mobile Devices:	N/A

Web Site: http://www.ppdi.com/

Mailing Address: Hansastrasse 32, 80686 Munchen, Germany

Telephone 1: +49 89 578770

Telephone 2: N/A

Fax: +49 89 57877400

Email: N/A

Country: **Germany**

Premier Research

EDC Products: Oracle Clinical Remote Data Capture

Services:

EDC:	Yes
eDiary/ePRO:	N/A
IVRS:	N/A
Mobile Devices:	N/A

Web Site: http://www.premier-research.com

Mailing Address: Birkenweg 14, D-64295 Darmstadt, Germany

Telephone 1: +49 (0) 6151 8280-0

Telephone 2: N/A

Fax: +49 (0) 6151 8280-10/-110

Email: N/A

Country: **Germany**

Quintegra Solutions GmbH

EDC Products: Quintegra's CDMS

Services:

EDC:	Yes
eDiary/ePRO:	N/A
IVRS:	N/A
Mobile Devices:	N/A

Web Site: htpp://www.quintegrasolutions.com/

Mailing Address: Stromberger Strasse 2, D-55545 Bad Kreuznach, Germany

Telephone 1: (+49) 671 920 275-1

Telephone 2: N/A

Fax: (+49) 671 920 275 - 9

Email: N/A

Country: **Germany**

StudyBuilder DE

EDC Products: StudyBuilder

Services:

    EDC: Yes

    eDiary/ePRO: Yes

    IVRS: N/A

    Mobile Devices: Yes

Web Site: www.studybuilder.de

Mailing Address: Abteilung   AA1146,   Postfach   100, 60545 Frankfurt, Germany

Telephone 1: +44 1865 338092

Telephone 2: N/A

Fax: +44 1865 338100

Email: de@studybuilder.com, info@studybuilder.de

Country: **Germany**

United Biosource Corporation

EDC Products: ClinPlus® Data Management System, SAS®-based

Services:

EDC:	Yes
eDiary/ePRO:	Yes
IVRS:	Yes
Mobile Devices:	Yes

Web Site: http://www.unitedbiosource.com

Mailing Address: Robert-Perthel-Str. 77a, D-50739 Cologne, Germany

Telephone 1: +49 221 59990

Telephone 2: N/A

Fax: +49 221 5999400

Email: info@unitedbiosource.com

Country: **Germany**

VIASYS Healthcare GmbH

EDC Products: Not specified

Services:

EDC:	Yes
eDiary/ePRO:	Yes
IVRS:	N/A
Mobile Devices:	Yes

Web Site: http://www.viasysclinical.com/

Mailing Address: Leibnizstrasse 7, 97204 Hoechberg, Germany

Telephone 1: + 49 931 4972 168

Telephone 2: N/A

Fax: + 49 931 4972 909

Email:
VCS.Business.development@viasyshc.com

Country: **Germany**

XClinical GmbH

EDC Products: MARVIN

Services:

EDC:	Yes
eDiary/ePRO:	N/A
IVRS:	N/A
Mobile Devices:	N/A

Web Site: http://www.xclinical.com

Mailing Address: Siegfriedstrasse 8, 80803 München, Germany

Telephone 1: +49 (0) 89 / 45 22 77 - 50 00

Telephone 2: N/A

Fax: +49 (0) 89 / 45 22 77 - 59 00

Email: info@xclinical.com

Greece

Country: **Greece**

PPD

EDC Products: Acceliant eClinical Suite, Oracle Clinical Remote Data Capture

Services:

EDC:	Yes
eDiary/ePRO:	N/A
IVRS:	Yes
Mobile Devices:	N/A

Web Site: http://www.ppdi.com/

Mailing Address: c/o Regus Athens, 166A, Kifissias Avenue & Sofokleous Street,Athens, GR-151 26 Maroussi, Greece

Telephone 1: +30 210 727 9064

Telephone 2: N/A

Fax: +30 210 727 9106

Email: N/A

Hungary

ICON Clinical Research

EDC Products: Medidata Rave™

Services:

EDC:	Yes
eDiary/ePRO:	N/A
IVRS:	N/A
Mobile Devices:	N/A

Web Site: htpp://www.iconclinical.com/

Mailing Address: Szépvölgyi út 39, Szépvölgyi Irodapark, 1037 Budapest, Hungary

Telephone 1: +36 1 430 4300

Telephone 2: N/A

Fax: +36 1 430 4330

Email: N/A

PPD

EDC Products: Acceliant eClinical Suite, Oracle Clinical Remote Data Capture

Services:

EDC:	Yes
eDiary/ePRO:	N/A
IVRS:	Yes
Mobile Devices:	N/A

Web Site: http://www.ppdi.com/

Mailing Address: Budapest, Dayka Gábor u. 3., H-1118 Hungary

Telephone 1: +36 1 248 4000

Telephone 2: N/A

Fax: +36 1 319 7513

Email: N/A

Country: **Hungary**

Premier Research

EDC Products: Oracle Clinical Remote Data Capture

Services:

EDC:	Yes
eDiary/ePRO:	N/A
IVRS:	N/A
Mobile Devices:	N/A

Web Site: http://www.premier-research.com

Mailing Address: Tölgyfa u. 24, H - 1027 Budapest, Hungary

Telephone 1: +36 1 460 9816

Telephone 2: N/A

Fax: +36 1 460 9815

Email: N/A

India

Country: **India**

Adobe Systems Incorporated

EDC Products: Adobe LiveCycle ES

Services:

EDC:	Yes
eDiary/ePRO:	N/A
IVRS:	N/A
Mobile Devices:	N/A

Web Site:
http://www.adobe.com/lifesciences/solutions/live cycle/

Mailing Address: Research and Development Pvt. Ltd., Salarpuria Infinity, 3rd Floor, #5, Bannerghatta Road, Bangalore-560029, India

Telephone 1: +91 80 4193 9500

Telephone 2: N/A

Fax: +91 80 4193 9505

Email: Use website for communication

Country: **India**

Afferenz

EDC Products: Acceliant Data Management, MedStudio

Services:

EDC:	Yes
eDiary/ePRO:	N/A
IVRS:	N/A
Mobile Devices:	N/A

Web Site: http://www.afferenz.com/

Mailing Address: 85 Kutchery Road, Mylapore, Chennai - 600 004, India

Telephone 1:   +91 44 2461 6768

Telephone 2:   N/A

Fax: +91 44 2461 7810

Email: afferenz-info@megasoft.com

Chiltern International Private Limited

EDC Products: Not specified

Services:

EDC:	Yes
eDiary/ePRO:	N/A
IVRS:	N/A
Mobile Devices:	N/A

Web Site: http://www2.chiltern.com/

Mailing Address: B Wing, 4th floor, Navkar Chambers Marol, Andheri Kurla Road, Andheri (E), Maharashtra, Mumbai, India

Telephone 1: +91 22 4098 2700

Telephone 2: N/A

Fax: +91 22 4098 2727

Email: N/A

Country: **India**

ICON Clinical Research

EDC Products: Medidata Rave™

Services:

EDC: Yes

eDiary/ePRO: N/A

IVRS: N/A

Mobile Devices: N/A

Web Site: htpp://www.iconclinical.com/

Mailing Address: Thiru & Thiru Chambers, No.31, opp Cannara Bank, Nandidurga Road, Bangalore, India, 560046

Telephone 1: +91 (80) 353 7675

Telephone 2: N/A

Fax: +91 (80) 354 0247

Email: info-India@iconcr.com

Paragon Biomedical, Inc.

<u>EDC Products:</u> Oracle Clinical® and ClinTrials™

<u>Services:</u>

        EDC: Yes

        eDiary/ePRO: N/A

        IVRS: Yes

        Mobile Devices: N/A

<u>Web Site:</u>   http://www.parabio.com

<u>Mailing Address:</u> B16, Gayatri, Technopark, Trivandrum—695 581, Kerala, India

<u>Telephone 1:</u> +91 47 1270 0094

<u>Telephone 2:</u> N/A

<u>Fax:</u>   +91 47 1270 0190

<u>Email:</u>   info@paragonbiomedical.com

Country: **India**

PPD

EDC Products: Acceliant eClinical Suite, Oracle Clinical Remote Data Capture

Services:

        EDC: Yes

        eDiary/ePRO: N/A

        IVRS: Yes

        Mobile Devices: N/A

Web Site: http://www.ppdi.com/

Mailing Address: 15th Floor, Eros Corporate Tower, Nehru Place, New Delhi 110 019, India

Telephone 1:   +91 11 4223 5337

Telephone 2:   N/A

Fax: +91 11 4223 5371

Email: N/A

Country: **India**

Progressive Life Sciences

EDC Products: In house solutions, combined with OpenClinica, SPSS, EpiInfo

Services:

EDC:	Yes
eDiary/ePRO:	N/A
IVRS:	N/A
Mobile Devices:	N/A

Web Site:
htpp://www.progressivelifesciences.com/

Mailing Address: 903, Arunachal building,Barakhamba Road, New Delhi, India

Telephone 1: +91 99 6829 5224

Telephone 2: N/A

Fax: + 91 11 2332 1509

Email: info@progressivelifesciences.com

Country: **India**

Quintegra Solutions Limited

EDC Products: Quintegra's CDMS

Services:

EDC:	Yes
eDiary/ePRO:	N/A
IVRS:	N/A
Mobile Devices:	N/A

Web Site: htpp://www.quintegrasolutions.com/

Mailing Address: 168, Eldams Road, Chennai - 600018, Tamilnadu, India

Telephone 1: +91 44 4391 7100

Telephone 2: N/A

Fax: +91 44 2432 8399

Email: N/A

Country: **India**

StudyBuilder Limited

EDC Products: StudyBuilder

Services:

EDC:	Yes
eDiary/ePRO:	Yes
IVRS:	N/A
Mobile Devices:	Yes

Web Site: www.studybuilder.in

Mailing Address: N/A

Telephone 1: +44 18 6533 8092

Telephone 2: N/A

Fax: +44 18 6533 8100

Email: in@studybuilder.com, info@studybuilder.in

Country: **India**

UNITHINK SERVICES Pvt. Ltd

EDC Products: UNITHINK EDC, UNITHINK eCRF

Services:

EDC:	Yes
eDiary/ePRO:	N/A
IVRS:	N/A
Mobile Devices:	N/A

Web Site: http://www.unithink.org/

Mailing Address: 01, Nutan Residency, 5-9-22/93, Adarsh Nagar, Hyderabad 500063, INDIA

Telephone 1: +91 40 2329 7743

Telephone 2: N/A

Fax: +91 40 2329 7743

Email: info@unithink.org

EDC Providers

Country: **India**

Ireland

Adobe Systems Software Ireland Limited

EDC Products: Adobe LiveCycle ES

Services:

EDC:	Yes
eDiary/ePRO:	N/A
IVRS:	N/A
Mobile Devices:	N/A

Web Site:
http://www.adobe.com/lifesciences/solutions/live cycle/

Mailing Address: 4-6 Riverwalk, Citywest Business Campus, Dublin 24, Ireland

Telephone 1: +353 1 242 6700

Telephone 2: N/A

Fax: +353 1 242 6711

Email: Use website for communication

Country: **Ireland**

Clinical Trial Endpoint Ltd.

EDC Products: CTEP's EDC system

Services:

EDC:	Yes
eDiary/ePRO:	N/A
IVRS:	N/A
Mobile Devices:	N/A

Web Site: http://www.ctep.eu/

Mailing Address: United Drug House, Magna Park, Citywest Road, Dublin 24, Ireland

Telephone 1: +353 1 463 7723

Telephone 2: N/A

Fax: +353 1 463 7785

Email: info@ctep.eu

Country: **Ireland**

ICON Clinical Research

EDC Products: Medidata Rave™

Services:

EDC:	Yes
eDiary/ePRO:	N/A
IVRS:	N/A
Mobile Devices:	N/A

Web Site: htpp://www.iconclinical.com/

Mailing Address: South County Business Park, Leopardstown, Dublin 18, Ireland

Telephone 1: +353 1 291 2000

Telephone 2: N/A

Fax: +353 1 291 2700

Email: N/A

Country: **Ireland**

StudyBuilder IE

EDC Products: StudyBuilder

Services:

EDC:	Yes
eDiary/ePRO:	Yes
IVRS:	N/A
Mobile Devices:	Yes

Web Site: www.studybuilder.ie

Mailing Address: Dept. AA1146, PO Box 4214, Dublin 2, Ireland

Telephone 1: +44 18 6533 8092

Telephone 2: N/A

Fax: +44 18 6533 8100

Email: ie@studybuilder.com, info@studybuilder.ie

EDC Providers

Country: **Ireland**

Israel

Harrison Clinical Research Israel L.P.

EDC Products: Marvin

Services:

        EDC: Yes

        eDiary/ePRO: Yes

        IVRS: N/A

        Mobile Devices: N/A

Web Site: http://www.harrisonclinical.com

Mailing Address: 10 Rehovot Science Park, Rehovot 76706, Israel

Telephone 1:   +9 72 8 931 6330

Telephone 2:   N/A

Fax: +972 8 931 6331

Email: N/A

ICON Clinical Research

EDC Products: Medidata Rave™

Services:

EDC:	Yes
eDiary/ePRO:	N/A
IVRS:	N/A
Mobile Devices:	N/A

Web Site: htpp://www.iconclinical.com/

Mailing Address: 6 Haba'al Shem Tov st., North Industrial Area Lod 71289, POB 1114 Lod 71100, Israel

Telephone 1: +972 8 915 2111

Telephone 2: N/A

Fax: +972 8 915 2333

Email: N/A

PPD

EDC Products: Acceliant eClinical Suite, Oracle Clinical Remote Data Capture

Services:

EDC:	Yes
eDiary/ePRO:	N/A
IVRS:	Yes
Mobile Devices:	N/A

Web Site: http://www.ppdi.com/

Mailing Address: Kiryat Atidim, Building No. 2, P.O. Box 58172, Tel Aviv 61580, Israel

Telephone 1: +972 3 768 8100

Telephone 2: N/A

Fax: +972 3 648 9994

Email: N/A

Italy

Country: **Italy**

Adobe Systems Italia Srl.

EDC Products: Adobe LiveCycle ES

Services:

EDC:	Yes
eDiary/ePRO:	N/A
IVRS:	N/A
Mobile Devices:	N/A

Web Site:
   http://www.adobe.com/lifesciences/solutions/live cycle/

Mailing Address: Viale Colleoni, 5, Centro Direzionale Colleoni, Palazzo Taurus A3, 20041 Agrate Brianza, Milano, Italy

Telephone 1:   +39 03 96 5501

Telephone 2:   N/A

Fax: +39 03 965 5050

Email: Use   website   for   communication

Country: **Italy**

Chiltern International Limited

EDC Products: Not specified

Services:

    EDC: Yes

    eDiary/ePRO: N/A

    IVRS: N/A

    Mobile Devices: N/A

Web Site: http://www2.chiltern.com/

Mailing Address: Via Nizzoli 6, 20147 Milan, Italy

Telephone 1:   +39 02 8907 8373

Telephone 2:   N/A

Fax: +39 02 4154 9832

Email: N/A

Harrison Clinical Research Italia S.r.l.

EDC Products: Marvin

Services:

EDC:	Yes
eDiary/ePRO:	Yes
IVRS:	N/A
Mobile Devices:	N/A

Web Site: http://www.harrisonclinical.com

Mailing Address: Via Antonio Vivaldi, 13, 00043 Ciampino, Rome, Italy

Telephone 1:   +39 06 7931 2131

Telephone 2:   N/A

Fax: +39 06 7931 2121

Email: N/A

ICON Clinical Research

EDC Products: Medidata Rave™

Services:

EDC:	Yes
eDiary/ePRO:	N/A
IVRS:	N/A
Mobile Devices:	N/A

Web Site: htpp://www.iconclinical.com/

Mailing Address: Via Washington, 70, Floor 2A, 20146 Milan, Italy

Telephone 1: +39 02 4657 1100

Telephone 2: N/A

Fax: +39 02 8058 1834

Email: N/A

PPD

EDC Products: Acceliant eClinical Suite, Oracle Clinical Remote Data Capture

Services:

EDC: Yes

eDiary/ePRO: N/A

IVRS: Yes

Mobile Devices: N/A

Web Site: http://www.ppdi.com/

Mailing Address: Palazzo Verrocchio, Centro Direzionale Milano Due, 20090 Segrate (Milano), Italy

Telephone 1: +39 02 21 0811

Telephone 2: N/A

Fax: +39 02 215 2912

Email: N/A

Country: **Italy**

Premier Research

<u>EDC Products:</u> Oracle Clinical Remote Data Capture

<u>Services:</u>

    EDC: Yes

    eDiary/ePRO: N/A

    IVRS: N/A

    Mobile Devices: N/A

<u>Web Site:</u>   http://www.premier-research.com

<u>Mailing Address:</u> Via Winckelmann 2, Milano 20146, Italy

<u>Telephone 1:</u>   +39 02 4895 8768

<u>Telephone 2:</u>   N/A

<u>Fax:</u>   +39 02 4895 8776

<u>Email:</u>   N/A

EDC Providers

Country: **Italy**

Japan

Country: **Japan**

Adobe Systems Co., Ltd.

EDC Products: Adobe LiveCycle ES

Services:

EDC:	Yes
eDiary/ePRO:	N/A
IVRS:	N/A
Mobile Devices:	N/A

Web Site:
http://www.adobe.com/lifesciences/solutions/live cycle/

Mailing Address: Gate City Osaki, East Tower, 1-11-2 Osaki, Shinagawa-ku, Tokyo 141-0032, Japan

Telephone 1: +81 3 5740 2400

Telephone 2: N/A

Fax: N/A

Email: Use website for communication

Asklep Inc.

EDC Products: Marvin (by XClinical)

Services:

EDC:	Yes
eDiary/ePRO:	Yes
IVRS:	N/A
Mobile Devices:	N/A

Web Site: http://www.asklep.co.jp/english/

Mailing Address: 3 Kanda-Neribeicho, Chiyoda-ku, Tokyo 101-8202, Japan

Telephone 1: +81 3 5294 5222

Telephone 2: N/A

Fax: +81 3 5294 5231

Email: N/A

Country: **Japan**

CMIC Co., Ltd.

EDC Products: InForm ™ and Clintrial ™

Services:

EDC: Yes

eDiary/ePRO: N/A

IVRS: N/A

Mobile Devices: N/A

Web Site: http://www.cmic.co.jp

Mailing Address: Kongo Bldg, 7-10-4 Nishigotanda, shinagawa-ku, Tokyo 141-0031, Japan

Telephone 1: +81 3 5745 7070

Telephone 2: N/A

Fax: +81 3 5745 7077

Email: information@cmic.co.jp

Harrison Clinical Research Japan

EDC Products: Marvin

Services:

EDC: Yes

eDiary/ePRO: Yes

IVRS: N/A

Mobile Devices: N/A

Web Site: http://www.harrisonclinical.com

Mailing Address: 1-23-18-305 Sengen Tsukuba-shi, Ibaraki, 305-0047, Japan

Telephone 1: +81 29 6851 6720

Telephone 2: +81 (0)80 3428 4872

Fax: +81 29 6851 6720

Email: N/A

ICON Clinical Research

EDC Products: Medidata Rave™

Services:

EDC:	Yes
eDiary/ePRO:	N/A
IVRS:	N/A
Mobile Devices:	N/A

Web Site: htpp://www.iconclinical.com/

Mailing Address: Asahiseimei Sunaga Bldg, 5F, 2-2-6 Nihonbashi-bakurocho, Chuo-ku, Tokyo, 103-0002 Japan

Telephone 1: +81 3 5847 7051

Telephone 2: N/A

Fax: +81 3 5847 7053

Email: info@iconaus.com.au

Country: **Japan**

Medidata Solutions

EDC Products: Medidata Rave®

Services:

EDC:	Yes
eDiary/ePRO:	N/A
IVRS:	N/A
Mobile Devices:	N/A

Web Site: http://www.mdsol.com

Mailing Address: SOWA Gotanda Building, 4th Floor, 2-7-18 Higashi-Gotanda, Shinagawa-ku, Tokyo, 141-0022, Japan

Telephone 1: +81 3 4588 0800

Telephone 2: N/A

Fax: +81 3 5795 0860

Email: N/A

EDC Providers

Country: **Japan**

Phase Forward Japan KK

EDC Products: InForm™, Clintrial™, WebSDM™

Services:

EDC:	Yes
eDiary/ePRO:	N/A
IVRS:	N/A
Mobile Devices:	N/A

Web Site: http://www.phaseforward.com

Mailing Address: Sanbancho Yayoikan 3Fl., 6-2, Sanban-cho, Chiyoda-ku, Tokyo 102-0075, Japan

Telephone 1: +81 3 5276 4372

Telephone 2: N/A

Fax: +81 3 5276 4384

Email: info.japan@phaseforward.com

Country: **Japan**

StudyBuilder JP

EDC Products: StudyBuilder

Services:

EDC:	Yes
eDiary/ePRO:	Yes
IVRS:	N/A
Mobile Devices:	Yes

Web Site: http://www.studybuilder.com/

Mailing Address: Level 11 Park West Building, 6-12-1 Nishi-Shinjuku, Shinjuku-ku Tokyo 160-0023, Japan

Telephone 1: +44 18 6533 8092

Telephone 2: N/A

Fax: +44 18 6533 8100

Email: jp@studybuilder.com

Korea

Country: **Korea**

Adobe Systems Incorporated

EDC Products: Adobe LiveCycle ES

Services:

EDC:	Yes
eDiary/ePRO:	N/A
IVRS:	N/A
Mobile Devices:	N/A

Web Site:
http://www.adobe.com/lifesciences/solutions/live cycle/

Mailing Address: 16F, A, Kyobo Kangnam Tower, 1303-22 Seocho-dong, Seocho-gu, Seoul, Korea 137-070

Telephone 1: +82 2 530 8000

Telephone 2: N/A

Fax: +82 2 530 8001

Email: Use website for communication

ICON Clinical Research

EDC Products: Medidata Rave™

Services:

EDC: Yes

eDiary/ePRO: N/A

IVRS: N/A

Mobile Devices: N/A

Web Site: htpp://www.iconclinical.com/

Mailing Address: 4th floor, Ildong, Pharmaceutical Building, 60 YangJae 1-dong, Seocho-gu, Seoul 137-733, Korea

Telephone 1: +82 70 7011 2831

Telephone 2: N/A

Fax: +82 2 554 3247

Email: info@iconaus.com.au

EDC Providers

Country: **Korea**

PPD

EDC Products: Acceliant eClinical Suite, Oracle Clinical Remote Data Capture

Services:

EDC:	Yes
eDiary/ePRO:	N/A
IVRS:	Yes
Mobile Devices:	N/A

Web Site: http://www.ppdi.com/

Mailing Address: 402, 4th Floor Keungil Tower, 677-25 Yeoksam-dong Gangnam-gu, Seoul 135-080 Korea

Telephone 1: +82 2 3490 1709

Telephone 2: N/A

Fax: +82 2 3490 1710

Email: N/A

Latvia

Country: **Latvia**

ICON Clinical Research

EDC Products: Medidata Rave™

Services:

EDC:	Yes
eDiary/ePRO:	N/A
IVRS:	N/A
Mobile Devices:	N/A

Web Site: htpp://www.iconclinical.com/

Mailing Address: Vienibas gatve 198, Riga LV-1058, Latvia, 1058

Telephone 1:   +371 (7860) 281

Telephone 2:   N/A

Fax: +371 (7860) 282

Email: N/A

Lithuania

Country: **Lithuania**

ICON Clinical Research

EDC Products: Medidata Rave™

Services:

EDC:	Yes
eDiary/ePRO:	N/A
IVRS:	N/A
Mobile Devices:	N/A

Web Site: htpp://www.iconclinical.com/

Mailing Address: Konstitucijos pr. 7, 09308 Vilnius, Lithuania

Telephone 1: +370 (5) 248 7755

Telephone 2: N/A

Fax: +370 (5) 248 7756

Email: N/A

Luxembourg

Country: **Luxembourg**

StudyBuilder LU

EDC Products: StudyBuilder

Services:

EDC:	Yes
eDiary/ePRO:	Yes
IVRS:	N/A
Mobile Devices:	Yes

Web Site: http://www.studybuilder.com/

Mailing Address: Dept. AA1146, L-1060 Luxembourg

Telephone 1: +44 18 6533 8092

Telephone 2: N/A

Fax: +44 18 6533 8100

Email: lu@studybuilder.com

Malaysia

Country: **Malaysia**

Quintegra Solutions (M) Sdn. Bhd.

EDC Products: Quintegra's CDMS

Services:

    EDC: Yes

    eDiary/ePRO: N/A

    IVRS: N/A

    Mobile Devices: N/A

Web Site: htpp://www.quintegrasolutions.com/

Mailing Address: Suite 2B-7-3, Plaza Sentral, Jalan Stesen Sentral 5, Kuala Lumpur Sentral, 50470, Kuala Lumpur, Malaysia

Telephone 1: 603 2261 4009

Telephone 2: 603 2261 4099

Fax: 603 2261 4199

Email: N/A

Mexico

ICON Clinical Research

EDC Products: Medidata Rave™

Services:

EDC:	Yes
eDiary/ePRO:	N/A
IVRS:	N/A
Mobile Devices:	N/A

Web Site: htpp://www.iconclinical.com/

Mailing Address: Av. Barranca del Muerto 329, 3rd Floor Mexico City, Mexico, 03900

Telephone 1: +52 55 5999 4666

Telephone 2: N/A

Fax: +52 55 5999 4633

Email: info@iconaus.com.au

PPD

EDC Products: Acceliant eClinical Suite, Oracle Clinical Remote Data Capture

Services:

EDC:	Yes
eDiary/ePRO:	N/A
IVRS:	Yes
Mobile Devices:	N/A

Web Site: http://www.ppdi.com/

Mailing Address: Av. Paseo de la Reforma, No. 505, Piso 37, Col. Cuauhtemoc, Deleg. Cuauhtemoc, C. P. 06500, Mexico City, Mexico

Telephone 1:   +52 55 5010 3636

Telephone 2:   N/A

Fax: +52 55 5020 5215

Email: N/A

StudyBuilder Limited

EDC Products: StudyBuilder

Services:

EDC:	Yes
eDiary/ePRO:	Yes
IVRS:	N/A
Mobile Devices:	Yes

Web Site: www.studybuilder.com/mx

Mailing Address: N/A

Telephone 1: +44 18 6533 8092

Telephone 2: N/A

Fax: +44 18 6533 8100

Email: mx@studybuilder.com

Netherlands

Country: **Netherlands**

Adobe Systems Benelux BV

<u>**EDC Products:**</u> Adobe LiveCycle ES

<u>**Services:**</u>

EDC:	Yes
eDiary/ePRO:	N/A
IVRS:	N/A
Mobile Devices:	N/A

<u>**Web Site:**</u>
http://www.adobe.com/lifesciences/solutions/live cycle/

<u>**Mailing Address:**</u> Europlaza, Hoogoorddreef 54a, 1101 BE Amsterdam ZO, The Netherlands

<u>**Telephone 1:**</u>   +31 20 651 1200

<u>**Telephone 2:**</u>   N/A

<u>**Fax:**</u>   +31 20 651 1300

<u>**Email:**</u>   Use   website   for   communication

Country: **Netherlands**

ICON Clinical Research

EDC Products: Medidata Rave™

Services:

EDC:	Yes
eDiary/ePRO:	N/A
IVRS:	N/A
Mobile Devices:	N/A

Web Site: htpp://www.iconclinical.com/

Mailing Address: Handelsweg 53, 1181 ZA, Amstelveen, Amsterdam, Netherlands

Telephone 1: +31 20 715 0000

Telephone 2: N/A

Fax: +31 20 715 0099

Email: N/A

Country: **Netherlands**

NovaXon B.V.

EDC Products: XClin Trials

Services:

EDC:	Yes
eDiary/ePRO:	N/A
IVRS:	N/A
Mobile Devices:	Yes

Web Site: htpp://www.novaxon.com/

Mailing Address: Sint Maartenslaan 26, 6221 AX Maastricht, The Netherlands

Telephone 1: +31 43 356 1460

Telephone 2: N/A

Fax: +31 43 356 1461

Email: info@novaxon.com

PPD

EDC Products: Acceliant eClinical Suite, Oracle Clinical Remote Data Capture

Services:

EDC:	Yes
eDiary/ePRO:	N/A
IVRS:	Yes
Mobile Devices:	N/A

Web Site: http://www.ppdi.com/

Mailing Address: Amsterdamseweg 34b-6712 GJ Ede, Postbus 548-6710 BM Ede, The Netherlands

Telephone 1: +31 31 865 8888

Telephone 2: N/A

Fax: +31 31 865 8800

Email: N/A

Country: **Netherlands**

StudyBuilder NL

EDC Products: StudyBuilder

Services:

EDC:	Yes
eDiary/ePRO:	Yes
IVRS:	N/A
Mobile Devices:	Yes

Web Site: http://www.studybuilder.com/

Mailing Address: Dept. AA1146, c/o RM Netherlands, Postbus 1048, 2800 CA Rijswijk, Netherlands

Telephone 1: +44 18 6533 8092

Telephone 2: N/A

Fax: +44 18 6533 8100

Email: nl@studybuilder.com

Country: **Netherlands**

Tessella Inc.

EDC Products: Adaptive Clinical Trials

Services:

EDC:	Yes
eDiary/ePRO:	Yes
IVRS:	N/A
Mobile Devices:	Yes

Web Site: http://www.tessella.com/

Mailing Address: Tauro   Kantorencentrum,   President Kennedylaan 19, 2517JK Den Haag, The Netherlands

Telephone 1:   +31 70 354 2296

Telephone 2:   N/A

Fax: +31 70 354 2296

Email: nfo@tessella.com

Country: **Netherlands**

Thorin BV

EDC Products: DataFax, iDataFax

Services:

 EDC: Yes

 eDiary/ePRO: N/A

 IVRS: N/A

 Mobile Devices: N/A

Web Site: http://www.thorin.nl/

Mailing Address: Rozemarijnstraat 1, 4451 TP Heinkenszand, The Netherlands

Telephone 1: +31 11 327 0259

Telephone 2: N/A

Fax: N/A

Email: info@thorin.nl

Country: **Netherlands**

VIASYS Healthcare, European Training Center

EDC Products: AM 2 + PEF Meter, AM 1 PEF Meter, VIAPAD eDiary

Services:

EDC:	N/A
eDiary/ePRO:	Yes
IVRS:	N/A
Mobile Devices:	Yes

Web Site: http://www.viasyshealthcare.com/

Mailing Address: De Molen 8-10, 3994 DB Houten, The Netherlands

Telephone 1: +31 30 228 9711

Telephone 2: N/A

Fax: +31 30 228 9713

Email: N/A

EDC Providers

Country: **Netherlands**

New Zealand

ICON Clinical Research

EDC Products: Medidata Rave™

Services:

EDC: Yes

eDiary/ePRO: N/A

IVRS: N/A

Mobile Devices: N/A

Web Site: htpp://www.iconclinical.com/

Mailing Address: Level 27, PWC Tower, 188 Quay Street, Auckland, New Zealand

Telephone 1: +64 (9) 363 2954

Telephone 2: N/A

Fax: +64 (9) 363 2756

Email: info@iconaus.com.au

Country: **New Zealand**

StudyBuilder NZ

<u>**EDC Products:**</u> StudyBuilder

<u>**Services:**</u>

      EDC: Yes

      eDiary/ePRO: Yes

      IVRS: N/A

      Mobile Devices: Yes

<u>**Web Site:**</u>   www.studybuilder.com/nz

<u>**Mailing Address:**</u> N/A

<u>**Telephone 1:**</u>   +44 18 6533 8092

<u>**Telephone 2:**</u>   N/A

<u>**Fax:**</u>   +44 18 6533 8100

<u>**Email:**</u>   nz@studybuilder.com

EDC Providers

Country: **New Zealand**

Norway

Adobe Systems Norge AS

EDC Products: Adobe LiveCycle ES

Services:

EDC:	Yes
eDiary/ePRO:	N/A
IVRS:	N/A
Mobile Devices:	N/A

Web Site:
http://www.adobe.com/lifesciences/solutions/live cycle/

Mailing Address: Jernbanetorget 2, Postboks 742, Sentrum, 0106 Oslo, Norge

Telephone 1: +47 2316 2881

Telephone 2: N/A

Fax: +47 2316 2882

Email: Use website for communication

Country: **Norway**

StudyBuilder NO

EDC Products: StudyBuilder

Services:

EDC:	Yes
eDiary/ePRO:	Yes
IVRS:	N/A
Mobile Devices:	Yes

Web Site: www.studybuilder.com/no

Mailing Address: N/A

Telephone 1: +44 18 6533 8092

Telephone 2: N/A

Fax: +44 18 6533 8100

Email: no@studybuilder.com

EDC Providers

Country: **Norway**

Peru

Country: **Peru**

ICON Clinical Research

EDC Products: Medidata Rave™

Services:

EDC:	Yes
eDiary/ePRO:	N/A
IVRS:	N/A
Mobile Devices:	N/A

Web Site: htpp://www.iconclinical.com/

Mailing Address: Av. 28 de Julio 150, Piso 6, Miraflores, Lima 18, Perú

Telephone 1: +51 1219 4100

Telephone 2: N/A

Fax: +51 1219 4110

Email: N/A

PPD

EDC Products: Acceliant eClinical Suite, Oracle Clinical Remote Data Capture

Services:

EDC:	Yes
eDiary/ePRO:	N/A
IVRS:	Yes
Mobile Devices:	N/A

Web Site: http://www.ppdi.com/

Mailing Address: Victor Andres Belaunde 147, Via principal 140, Edificio Real Seis, Piso 7, Centro Empresarial Real – San Isidro, Lima 27 – Perú

Telephone 1: +51 1211 2618

Telephone 2: N/A

Fax: +51 1211 2752

Email: N/A

EDC Providers

Country: **Peru**

Poland

Country: **Poland**

Accovion Sp. z o.o.

EDC Products: Oracle Clinical, Clintrial

Services:

EDC:	Yes
eDiary/ePRO:	Yes
IVRS:	N/A
Mobile Devices:	N/A

Web Site: http://www.accovion.com/

Mailing Address: Al. Jana Pawla II 23, 00-854 Warszawa, Poland

Telephone 1: +48 29 758 1504

Telephone 2: N/A

Fax: +48 29 758 1508

Email: magdalena.kozak@accovion.com

Country: **Poland**

Chiltern International Limited

<u>EDC Products:</u> Not specified

<u>Services:</u>

EDC:	Yes
eDiary/ePRO:	N/A
IVRS:	N/A
Mobile Devices:	N/A

<u>Web Site:</u>   http://www2.chiltern.com/

<u>Mailing Address:</u> Ursynow Business Park, ul. Pulawska 303, 02-785 Warsaw, Poland

<u>Telephone 1:</u>   +48 22 549 4330

<u>Telephone 2:</u>   N/A

<u>Fax:</u>   +48 22 549 4331

<u>Email:</u>   N/A

Harrison Clinical Research Poland

EDC Products: Marvin

Services:

EDC: Yes

eDiary/ePRO: Yes

IVRS: N/A

Mobile Devices: N/A

Web Site: http://www.harrisonclinical.com

Mailing Address: ul. Krucza 16/22, 00-526 Warszawa, Poland

Telephone 1: +48 22 434 2660

Telephone 2: N/A

Fax: +48 22 434 2664

Email: N/A

Country: **Poland**

ICON Clinical Research

EDC Products: Medidata Rave™

Services:

EDC:	Yes
eDiary/ePRO:	N/A
IVRS:	N/A
Mobile Devices:	N/A

Web Site: htpp://www.iconclinical.com/

Mailing Address: Ul. Grójecka 5, 02-019, Warszawa, Poland

Telephone 1:   +48 22 451 6310

Telephone 2:   N/A

Fax: +48 22 451 6311

Email: N/A

Country: **Poland**

Paragon Biomedical, Inc.

EDC Products: Oracle Clinical® and ClinTrials™

Services:

EDC:	Yes
eDiary/ePRO:	N/A
IVRS:	Yes
Mobile Devices:	N/A

Web Site: http://www.parabio.com

Mailing Address: Ul. Chalubinskiego 8, Floor 40, 00-613 Warsaw, Poland

Telephone 1: +48 22 830 1424

Telephone 2: N/A

Fax: +48 22 830 1422

Email: info@paragonbiomedical.com

PPD

EDC Products: Acceliant eClinical Suite, Oracle Clinical Remote Data Capture

Services:

EDC:	Yes
eDiary/ePRO:	N/A
IVRS:	Yes
Mobile Devices:	N/A

Web Site: http://www.ppdi.com/

Mailing Address: Budynek Orion, ul Postepu 18B, 02-676 Warszawa, Polska

Telephone 1:   +48 22 542 7000

Telephone 2:   N/A

Fax: +48 22 542 7500

Email: N/A

Country: **Poland**

Premier Research

<u>EDC Products:</u> Oracle Clinical Remote Data Capture

<u>Services:</u>

EDC: Yes

eDiary/ePRO: N/A

IVRS: N/A

Mobile Devices: N/A

<u>Web Site:</u> http://www.premier-research.com

<u>Mailing Address:</u> Premier Research Poland Sp. z.o.o.., ul. Pulawska 303, 02-785 Warszawa, Poland

<u>Telephone 1:</u> +48 22 549 4400

<u>Telephone 2:</u> N/A

<u>Fax:</u> +48 22 549 4410

<u>Email:</u> N/A

Country: **Portugal**

Portugal

Country: **Portugal**

Chiltern International Limited

EDC Products: Not specified

Services:

EDC: Yes

eDiary/ePRO: N/A

IVRS: N/A

Mobile Devices: N/A

Web Site: http://www2.chiltern.com/

Mailing Address: Galerias Alto da Barra, Avenida das Descobertas, 59-Piso 3, 2780-053 Oeiras, Portugal

Telephone 1: N/A

Telephone 2: N/A

Fax: N/A

Email: N/A

Country: **Portugal**

PPD

EDC Products: Acceliant eClinical Suite, Oracle Clinical Remote Data Capture

Services:

EDC:	Yes
eDiary/ePRO:	N/A
IVRS:	Yes
Mobile Devices:	N/A

Web Site: http://www.ppdi.com/

Mailing Address: Avenida da Liberdade, 110-1, 1269-046 Lisbon, Portugal

Telephone 1: +35 12 1340 4672

Telephone 2: N/A

Fax: +35 12 1340 4673

Email: N/A

Country: **Portugal**

StudyBuilder PT

<u>**EDC Products:**</u> StudyBuilder

<u>**Services:**</u>

          EDC: Yes

          eDiary/ePRO: Yes

          IVRS: N/A

          Mobile Devices: Yes

<u>**Web Site:**</u>   http://www.studybuilder.com/

<u>**Mailing Address:**</u> Dept. AA1146, Apartado 8075, 1801-001 Lisboa, Portugal

<u>**Telephone 1:**</u>   +44 18 6533 8092

<u>**Telephone 2:**</u>   N/A

<u>**Fax:**</u>   +44 18 6533 8100

<u>**Email:**</u>   pt@studybuilder.com

Romania

ICON Clinical Research

EDC Products: Medidata Rave™

Services:

EDC:	Yes
eDiary/ePRO:	N/A
IVRS:	N/A
Mobile Devices:	N/A

Web Site: htpp://www.iconclinical.com/

Mailing Address: Floreasca Business Center, 133-137 Calea Floreasca St., 014456 Bucharest, Romania

Telephone 1: + 40 21 264 8300

Telephone 2: N/A

Fax: + 40 21 264 8399

Email: N/A

Premier Research

<u>EDC Products:</u> Oracle Clinical Remote Data Capture

<u>Services:</u>

EDC: Yes

eDiary/ePRO: N/A

IVRS: N/A

Mobile Devices: N/A

<u>Web Site:</u> http://www.premier-research.com

<u>Mailing Address:</u> Diplomat Business Center, Sevastopol Street, No. 13-17, Ap. 111, Sector 1, RO-010991 Bucharest, Romania

<u>Telephone 1:</u> +40 21 310 6537

<u>Telephone 2:</u> N/A

<u>Fax:</u> +40 21 310 6535

<u>Email:</u> N/A

EDC Providers

Country: **Romania**

Russia

ClinResearch GmbH

EDC Products: Oracle-based data management system

Services:

EDC:	Yes
eDiary/ePRO:	N/A
IVRS:	N/A
Mobile Devices:	N/A

Web Site: http://www.clinresearch.com/

Mailing Address: Varshavskaoye shosse 17, bldg. 1, office 113, 117105 Moscow, Russia

Telephone 1: +7 495 788 9807

Telephone 2: N/A

Fax: +7 495 788 9817

Email: N/A

Country: **Russia**

Harrison Clinical Research Russia

EDC Products: Marvin

Services:

EDC:	Yes
eDiary/ePRO:	Yes
IVRS:	N/A
Mobile Devices:	N/A

Web Site: http://www.harrisonclinical.com

Mailing Address: Academica Pilyugina Str. 14, bldg. 3, app. 976-979, 117393, Moscow, Russia

Telephone 1: +7 495 514 1392

Telephone 2: N/A

Fax: +7 495 939 2430

Email: N/A

Country: **Russia**

ICON Clinical Research

EDC Products: Medidata Rave™

Services:

EDC:	Yes
eDiary/ePRO:	N/A
IVRS:	N/A
Mobile Devices:	N/A

Web Site: htpp://www.iconclinical.com/

Mailing Address: Smonlnaya str, bld. 24D, Meridian Commercial Tower, 125445 Moscow, Russia

Telephone 1: +7 495 540 4124

Telephone 2: N/A

Fax: +7 495 540 4125

Email: N/A

Country: **Russia**

Premier Research

EDC Products: Oracle Clinical Remote Data Capture

Services:

EDC:	Yes
eDiary/ePRO:	N/A
IVRS:	N/A
Mobile Devices:	N/A

Web Site: http://www.premier-research.com

Mailing Address: Office 527, block 11, 3 Gostinichinaya str., RUS-127106, Moscow, Russia

Telephone 1: +7 095 772 9845

Telephone 2: N/A

Fax: +7 095 772 9845

Email: N/A

Country: **Russia**

United Biosource Corporation

EDC Products: ClinPlus® Data Management System, SAS®-based

Services:

EDC:	Yes
eDiary/ePRO:	Yes
IVRS:	Yes
Mobile Devices:	Yes

Web Site: http://www.unitedbiosource.com

Mailing Address: Varshavskaoye shosse 17, bldg. 1, office 113, 117105 Moscow, Russia

Telephone 1: +007 495 788 9807

Telephone 2:

Fax: +007 495 788 9817

Email: info@unitedbiosource.com

Singapore

Country: **Singapore**

Adobe Systems Incorporated

<u>EDC Products:</u> Adobe LiveCycle ES

<u>Services:</u>

EDC:	Yes
eDiary/ePRO:	N/A
IVRS:	N/A
Mobile Devices:	N/A

<u>Web Site:</u>
http://www.adobe.com/lifesciences/solutions/livecycle/

<u>Mailing Address:</u> No. 8 Temasek Boulevard Suntec Tower 3, #06-02, Singapore 038988

<u>Telephone 1:</u>   +65 6511 5500

<u>Telephone 2:</u>   N/A

<u>Fax:</u>   +65 6333 8023

<u>Email:</u>   Use   website   for   communication

Country: **Singapore**

ICON Clinical Research

EDC Products: Medidata Rave™

Services:

EDC: Yes

eDiary/ePRO: N/A

IVRS: N/A

Mobile Devices: N/A

Web Site: htpp://www.iconclinical.com/

Mailing Address: 1 International Business Park, 03-01A The Synergy Tower Block, Singapore 609917, Republic of Singapore

Telephone 1:   +65 6896 2538

Telephone 2:   N/A

Fax: +65 6896 2438

Email: info@iconaus.com.au

Country: **Singapore**

PPD

EDC Products: Acceliant eClinical Suite, Oracle Clinical Remote Data Capture

Services:

EDC:	Yes
eDiary/ePRO:	N/A
IVRS:	Yes
Mobile Devices:	N/A

Web Site: http://www.ppdi.com/

Mailing Address: 10 Science Park Road, #02-04 The Alpha, Singapore Science Park II, Singapore 117684

Telephone 1: +65 6872 3588

Telephone 2: N/A

Fax: +65 6872 3522

Email: N/A

Country: **Singapore**

Quintegra Solutions Pte. Ltd.

EDC Products: Quintegra's CDMS

Services:

EDC:	Yes
eDiary/ePRO:	N/A
IVRS:	N/A
Mobile Devices:	N/A

Web Site: htpp://www.quintegrasolutions.com/

Mailing Address: 70 Shenton Way, #20-01 Marina House, Singapore 079118

Telephone 1: +65 6837 1538

Telephone 2: N/A

Fax: + 65 6837 1539

Email: N/A

Country: **Singapore**

SGS Singapore

<u>EDC Products:</u> Phase Forward InForm

<u>Services:</u>

EDC:	Yes
eDiary/ePRO:	N/A
IVRS:	N/A
Mobile Devices:	N/A

<u>Web Site:</u>   http://www.clinicalresearch.sgs.com

<u>Mailing Address:</u> Ayer Rajah Crescent #03-07, Ayer Rajah Industrial Estate, 139944 Singapore

<u>Telephone 1:</u>   +65 6775 3034

<u>Telephone 2:</u>   N/A

<u>Fax:</u>   N/A

<u>Email:</u>   N/A

Slovak Republic

EDC Providers

Country: **Slovak Republic**

Premier Research

<u>EDC Products:</u> Oracle Clinical Remote Data Capture

<u>Services:</u>

EDC: Yes

eDiary/ePRO: N/A

IVRS: N/A

Mobile Devices: N/A

<u>Web Site:</u> http://www.premier-research.com

<u>Mailing Address:</u> Udernicka 5, SK-85102 Bratislava, Slovak Republic

<u>Telephone 1:</u> +421 2 682 0608-1

<u>Telephone 2:</u> N/A

<u>Fax:</u> +421 2 682 0608-0

<u>Email:</u> N/A

South Africa

Country: **South Africa**

Adobe Systems South Africa (Pty) Ltd

EDC Products: Adobe LiveCycle ES

Services:

EDC:	Yes
eDiary/ePRO:	N/A
IVRS:	N/A
Mobile Devices:	N/A

Web Site:
http://www.adobe.com/lifesciences/solutions/livecycle/

Mailing Address: West Wing, Birchwood Court, 43 Montrose Street, Midrand, 1686, South Africa

Telephone 1: +27 11 655 7192

Telephone 2: N/A

Fax: +27 11 655 7011

Email: Use website for communication

Country: **South Africa**

ICON Clinical Research

EDC Products: Medidata Rave™

Services:

EDC:	Yes
eDiary/ePRO:	N/A
IVRS:	N/A
Mobile Devices:	N/A

Web Site: htpp://www.iconclinical.com/

Mailing Address: Block 6, Harrowdene Office Park, Western Service Road, Woodmead, Johannesburg, South Africa

Telephone 1: +27 11 209 1100

Telephone 2: N/A

Fax: +27 11 802 0490

Email: info@iconaus.com.au

Country: **South Africa**

PPD

EDC Products: Acceliant eClinical Suite, Oracle Clinical Remote Data Capture

Services:

EDC:	Yes
eDiary/ePRO:	N/A
IVRS:	Yes
Mobile Devices:	N/A

Web Site: http://www.ppdi.com/

Mailing Address: The Woodlands Office Park, P.O. Box 37, Woodmead 2080, Johannesburg, South Africa

Telephone 1: +27 11 612 8600

Telephone 2: N/A

Fax: +27 11 612 8601

Email: N/A

Country: **South Africa**

StudyBuilder Limited

<u>EDC Products:</u> StudyBuilder

<u>Services:</u>

EDC:	Yes
eDiary/ePRO:	Yes
IVRS:	N/A
Mobile Devices:	Yes

<u>Web Site:</u> www.studybuilder.com/za

<u>Mailing Address:</u> N/A

<u>Telephone 1:</u> +44 18 6533 8092

<u>Telephone 2:</u> N/A

<u>Fax:</u> +44 18 6533 8100

<u>Email:</u> za@studybuilder.com

EDC Providers

Country: **South Africa**

Spain

Country: **Spain**

Adobe Systems Iberica, S.L

EDC Products: Adobe LiveCycle ES

Services:

EDC:	Yes
eDiary/ePRO:	N/A
IVRS:	N/A
Mobile Devices:	N/A

Web Site:
http://www.adobe.com/lifesciences/solutions/livecycle/

Mailing Address: Torre Mapfre — Villa Olimpica Marina, 16-18 Planta 20, 08005, Barcelona, España

Telephone 1: +34 93 326 8400

Telephone 2: N/A

Fax: +34 93 326 8420

Email: Use website for communication

Country: **Spain**

Chiltern International Limited

<u>**EDC Products:**</u> Not specified

<u>**Services:**</u>

    EDC: Yes

    eDiary/ePRO: N/A

    IVRS: N/A

    Mobile Devices: N/A

<u>**Web Site:**</u>   http://www2.chiltern.com/

<u>**Mailing Address:**</u> Centro Empresarial Euronova 3, Ronda de Poniente, 10-2, 28760 Tres Cantos, Madrid, Spain

<u>**Telephone 1:**</u>   +34 91 187 2700

<u>**Telephone 2:**</u>   N/A

<u>**Fax:**</u>   +34 91 187 2849

<u>**Email:**</u>   N/A

Harrison Clinical Research Iberica

EDC Products: Marvin

Services:

EDC:	Yes
eDiary/ePRO:	Yes
IVRS:	N/A
Mobile Devices:	N/A

Web Site: http://www.harrisonclinical.com

Mailing Address: Calle Princep Jordi, 21-23, Esc.B, Entresol 1 B, 08014 Barselona, Spain

Telephone 1:   +34 93 226 6964

Telephone 2:   N/A

Fax: +34 93 226 5833

Email: N/A

Country: **Spain**

ICON Clinical Research

EDC Products: Medidata Rave™

Services:

EDC:	Yes
eDiary/ePRO:	N/A
IVRS:	N/A
Mobile Devices:	N/A

Web Site: htpp://www.iconclinical.com/

Mailing Address: Torre Diagonal Mar, Piso 11, Modulo A1, C/Josep Pla n°2, 08019 Barcelona, Spain

Telephone 1: +34 93 489 8500

Telephone 2: N/A

Fax: +34 93 356 1371

Email: N/A

Country: **Spain**

PPD

EDC Products: Acceliant eClinical Suite, Oracle Clinical Remote Data Capture

Services:

EDC:	Yes
eDiary/ePRO:	N/A
IVRS:	Yes
Mobile Devices:	N/A

Web Site: http://www.ppdi.com/

Mailing Address: 2nd Floor, Paseo de la Castellana 4, Madrid, 28046, Spain

Telephone 1: +34 91 567 2320

Telephone 2: N/A

Fax: +34 91 571 6484

Email: N/A

Premier Research

<u>EDC Products:</u> Oracle Clinical Remote Data Capture

<u>Services:</u>

EDC: Yes

eDiary/ePRO: N/A

IVRS: N/A

Mobile Devices: N/A

<u>Web Site:</u> http://www.premier-research.com

<u>Mailing Address:</u> C/Musgo 5, 28023 Madrid, Spain

<u>Telephone 1:</u> +34 91 708 0386

<u>Telephone 2:</u> N/A

<u>Fax:</u> +34 91 708 0387

<u>Email:</u> N/A

SGS Life Science Services

EDC Products: Phase Forward InForm

Services:

EDC:	Yes
eDiary/ePRO:	N/A
IVRS:	N/A
Mobile Devices:	N/A

Web Site: http://www.clinicalresearch.sgs.com

Mailing Address: C/Trespaderne, 29 Edificio, Barajas 1, 28042 Madrid, Spain

Telephone 1: +34 93 467 8400

Telephone 2: N/A

Fax: N/A

Email: N/A

Country: **Spain**

StudyBuilder ES

EDC Products: StudyBuilder

Services:

EDC:	Yes
eDiary/ePRO:	Yes
IVRS:	N/A
Mobile Devices:	Yes

Web Site: www.studybuilder.es

Mailing Address: Dept. AA1146, Apdo de correso 1713, 28080 - MADRID, Spain

Telephone 1: +44 18 6533 8092

Telephone 2: N/A

Fax: +44 18 6533 8100

Email: es@studybuilder.com, info@studybuilder.es

EDC Providers

Country: **Spain**

Sweden

Country: **Sweden**

Adobe Systems Nordic AB.

EDC Products: Adobe LiveCycle ES

Services:

EDC:	Yes
eDiary/ePRO:	N/A
IVRS:	N/A
Mobile Devices:	N/A

Web Site:
http://www.adobe.com/lifesciences/solutions/live cycle/

Mailing Address: Finlandsgatan 16 Box 47 164 93, Kista, Sweden

Telephone 1: +46 8 752 3300

Telephone 2: N/A

Fax: +46 8 751 4955

Email: Use website for communication

Country: **Sweden**

ICON Clinical Research

EDC Products: Medidata Rave™

Services:

EDC:	Yes
eDiary/ePRO:	N/A
IVRS:	N/A
Mobile Devices:	N/A

Web Site: htpp://www.iconclinical.com/

Mailing Address: Gårdsvägen 18, PO Box 728, 16927 Solna, Sweden

Telephone 1: +46 8 514 84700

Telephone 2: N/A

Fax: +46 8 514 84702

Email: N/A

Country: **Sweden**

PPD

EDC Products: Acceliant eClinical Suite, Oracle Clinical Remote Data Capture

Services:

EDC: Yes

eDiary/ePRO: N/A

IVRS: Yes

Mobile Devices: N/A

Web Site: http://www.ppdi.com/

Mailing Address: Hälsingegatan 49, SE-113 31 Stockholm, Sweden

Telephone 1: +46 8 598 22400

Telephone 2: N/A

Fax: +46 8 598 22444

Email: N/A

Country: **Sweden**

StudyBuilder SE

EDC Products: StudyBuilder

Services:

EDC:	Yes
eDiary/ePRO:	Yes
IVRS:	N/A
Mobile Devices:	Yes

Web Site: http://www.studybuilder.com/

Mailing Address: Dept. AA1146, U410, SE-202 28 Malmö, Sweden

Telephone 1: +44 18 6533 8092

Telephone 2: N/A

Fax: +44 18 6533 8100

Email: se@studybuilder.com

EDC Providers

Country: **Sweden**

Switzerland

Country: **Switzerland**

Datagen, Ltd.

EDC Products: Custom built EDC systems

Services:

EDC:	Yes
eDiary/ePRO:	N/A
IVRS:	N/A
Mobile Devices:	N/A

Web Site: http://www.datagen.net/

Mailing Address: Information Management, Carl Güntert-Strasse 13a, CH-4310 Rheinfelden, Switzerland

Telephone 1: +41 61 831 7520

Telephone 2: N/A

Fax: +41 61 831 7520

Email: info@datagen.net

Country: **Switzerland**

Outcome Sciences, Inc.

EDC Products: Outcome System®, Outcome Offline™

Services:

EDC:	Yes
eDiary/ePRO:	Yes
IVRS:	Yes
Mobile Devices:	Yes

Web Site: http://www.outcome.com/

Mailing Address: Ch Du Canal 5, 1260 Nyon, Switzerland

Telephone 1: +41 22 361 8608

Telephone 2: +800 688 266 37 (+800 OUTCOMES)

Fax: +800 688 266 33

Email: info@outcome.com

PHT Corporation Sàrl

EDC   Products: ePRO   Product   Suite: LogPad System,StudyPad   System,eSense   Sensors, StudyWorks, Study Archive, ePRO Designer.

Services:

EDC:	Yes
eDiary/ePRO:	Yes
IVRS:	N/A
Mobile Devices:	Yes

Web Site: http://www.phtcorp.com

Mailing Address: 2, chemin Louis-Hubert, 1213 Petit-Lancy, Geneva, Switzerland

Telephone 1:   +41 22 879 9100

Telephone 2:   N/A

Fax: 41 22 879 9101

Email: N/A

Premier Research

<u>EDC Products:</u> Oracle Clinical Remote Data Capture

<u>Services:</u>

EDC: Yes

eDiary/ePRO: N/A

IVRS: N/A

Mobile Devices: N/A

<u>Web Site:</u> http://www.premier-research.com

<u>Mailing Address:</u> En Chamard 55C, 1442, Montagny-près-Yverdon, Switzerland

<u>Telephone 1:</u> +41 24 424 2688

<u>Telephone 2:</u> N/A

<u>Fax:</u> +41 24 424 2699

<u>Email:</u> N/A

Country: **Switzerland**

StudyBuilder CH

EDC Products: StudyBuilder

Services:

        EDC: Yes

        eDiary/ePRO: Yes

        IVRS: N/A

        Mobile Devices: Yes

Web Site: www.studybuilder.com/ch

Mailing Address: Dept. AA1146, Case Postale 1000, 1240 Genève 40, Switzerland

Telephone 1:   +44 18 6533 8092

Telephone 2:   N/A

Fax: +44 18 6533 8100

Email: ch@studybuilder.com, info@studybuilder.ch

Thailand

ICON Clinical Research

EDC Products: Medidata Rave™

Services:

EDC:	Yes
eDiary/ePRO:	N/A
IVRS:	N/A
Mobile Devices:	N/A

Web Site: htpp://www.iconclinical.com/

Mailing Address: Q House Lumpini, 1 South Sathorn Rd., Level 27, Tungmahamek, Sathorn, Bangkok, Thailand, 10120

Telephone 1: +662 610 3671-4

Telephone 2: N/A

Fax: +662 610 3882

Email: info@iconaus.com.au

PPD

<u>EDC Products:</u> Acceliant eClinical Suite, Oracle Clinical Remote Data Capture

<u>Services:</u>

EDC:	Yes
eDiary/ePRO:	N/A
IVRS:	Yes
Mobile Devices:	N/A

<u>Web Site:</u> http://www.ppdi.com/

<u>Mailing Address:</u> The Offices at Central World, 25th Floor, 999/9 Rama I Road, Patumwan, Bangkok 10330, Thailand

<u>Telephone 1:</u> +662 646 2100

<u>Telephone 2:</u> N/A

<u>Fax:</u> +662 646 1089

<u>Email:</u> N/A

EDC Providers

Country: **Thailand**

280

Turkey

Country: **Turkey**

PPD

EDC Products: Acceliant eClinical Suite, Oracle Clinical Remote Data Capture

Services:

EDC:	Yes
eDiary/ePRO:	N/A
IVRS:	Yes
Mobile Devices:	N/A

Web Site: http://www.ppdi.com/

Mailing Address: Perdemsac Plaza, Bayar Caddesi, Gülbahar Sokak 17, Kat: 10 106-107-108-109, Kozyatagi 34742, Istanbul, Turkey

Telephone 1: +90 216 571 4700

Telephone 2: N/A

Fax: +90 216 571 4720

Email: N/A

EDC Providers

Country: **Ukraine**

Ukraine

283

Country: **Ukraine**

Chiltern International Limited

EDC Products: Not specified

Services:

        EDC: Yes

        eDiary/ePRO: N/A

        IVRS: N/A

        Mobile Devices: N/A

Web Site: http://www2.chiltern.com/

Mailing Address: 18-22, Metalistiv Str., block 7, Kyiv, 03057, Ukraine

Telephone 1:   +38 044 593 6590

Telephone 2:   N/A

Fax: +380 44 593 6591

Email: N/A

ClinResearch GmbH

EDC Products: Oracle-based data management system

Services:

EDC:	Yes
eDiary/ePRO:	N/A
IVRS:	N/A
Mobile Devices:	N/A

Web Site: http://www.clinresearch.com/

Mailing Address: 12, Muzeynyi proulok, 4th floor, office 413, 01601 Kyiv (Kiev), Ukraine

Telephone 1: +38 044 253 6403

Telephone 2: N/A

Fax: +38 044 253 6340

Email: Use website for communication.

Harrison Clinical Research Ukraine

EDC Products: Marvin

Services:

EDC:	Yes
eDiary/ePRO:	Yes
IVRS:	N/A
Mobile Devices:	N/A

Web Site: http://www.harrisonclinical.com

Mailing Address: 30a Lisna str., Pushcha Voditsa, Kiev 04075, Ukraine

Telephone 1: +38 044 431 9836

Telephone 2: +38 044 431 9838

Fax: +38 044 431 9834

Email: N/A

Country: **Ukraine**

ICON Clinical Research

EDC Products: Medidata Rave™

Services:

EDC:	Yes
eDiary/ePRO:	N/A
IVRS:	N/A
Mobile Devices:	N/A

Web Site: htpp://www.iconclinical.com/

Mailing Address: St. Poleva, 24, Kiev, Ukraine, 03056

Telephone 1: +38 044 583 5600

Telephone 2: N/A

Fax: +38 044 583 5697

Email: N/A

Premier Research

<u>EDC Products:</u> Oracle Clinical Remote Data Capture

<u>Services:</u>

EDC: Yes

eDiary/ePRO: N/A

IVRS: N/A

Mobile Devices: N/A

<u>Web Site:</u> http://www.premier-research.com

<u>Mailing Address:</u> 2_B Mikilsko-Slobodska Str., Section N5, Office 273-273 A, UA-02002 Kiev, Ukraine

<u>Telephone 1:</u> +38 044 541 1155

<u>Telephone 2:</u> N/A

<u>Fax:</u> +38 044 541 1464

<u>Email:</u> N/A

United Biosource Corporation

EDC Products: ClinPlus® Data Management System, SAS®-based

Services:

EDC:	Yes
eDiary/ePRO:	Yes
IVRS:	Yes
Mobile Devices:	Yes

Web Site: http://www.unitedbiosource.com

Mailing Address: 12, Muzeynyi proulok, 4th floor, office 413, 01601 Kyiv (Kiev), Ukraine

Telephone 1: +38 044 253 6403

Telephone 2: N/A

Fax: +38 044 253 6340

Email: info@unitedbiosource.com

EDC Providers

Country: **Ukraine**

United Kingdom

Country: **United Kingdom**

Adobe Systems Europe Ltd

EDC Products: Adobe LiveCycle ES

Services:

EDC:	Yes
eDiary/ePRO:	N/A
IVRS:	N/A
Mobile Devices:	N/A

Web Site:
http://www.adobe.com/lifesciences/solutions/live cycle/

Mailing Address: 3 Roundwood Avenue, Stockley Park, Uxbridge, UB11 1AY, United Kingdom

Telephone 1: +44 (0) 208 606 1100

Telephone 2: N/A

Fax: +44 (0) 208 606 4004

Email: Use website for communication

Country: **United Kingdom**

Axiope Limited

EDC Products: e-CAT

Services:

EDC:	Yes
eDiary/ePRO:	Yes
IVRS:	N/A
Mobile Devices:	N/A

Web Site: http://www.axiope.com/oidex.html

Mailing Address: 24 Fountainhall Road, Edinburgh, EH9 2LW, UK

Telephone 1: +44 131 668 3232

Telephone 2: N/A

Fax: +44 871 251 4870

Email: info@axiope.com

Country: **United Kingdom**

Chiltern International Limited

EDC Products: Not specified

Services:

EDC:	Yes
eDiary/ePRO:	N/A
IVRS:	N/A
Mobile Devices:	N/A

Web Site: http://www2.chiltern.com/

Mailing Address: 171 Bath Road, Slough, Berkshire, SL1 4AA, UK

Telephone 1: +44 (0) 175 351 2000

Telephone 2: N/A

Fax: +44 (0) 175 351 1116

Email: N/A

Country: **United Kingdom**

Clinical Systems Ltd.

EDC Products: ClinAxys

Services:

EDC:	Yes
eDiary/ePRO:	N/A
IVRS:	N/A
Mobile Devices:	N/A

Web Site: http://www.clinaxys.com/

Mailing Address: 63 High Street, Princes Risborough, Buckinghamshire, HP27 0AE, United Kingdom

Telephone 1: +44 (0) 184 434 2490

Telephone 2: N/A

Fax: +44 (0) 184 434 2940

Email: enquiries@clinical-systems.co.uk

Country: **United Kingdom**

ClinPhone Plc.

EDC Products: ClinPhone Combined EDC-IVR: DataLabs by ClinPhone (EDC/CDMS) and ClinPhone IVR/IWR

Services:

EDC:	Yes
eDiary/ePRO:	Yes
IVRS:	Yes
Mobile Devices:	N/A

Web Site: http://www.clinphone.com

Mailing Address: Lady Bay House, Meadow Grove, Nottingham, NG2 3HF, UK

Telephone 1: +44 115 955 7333

Telephone 2: N/A

Fax: +44 115 955 7555

Email: info@clinphone.com

Country: **United Kingdom**

Cmed Group Limited

EDC Products: Timaeus (formerly known as ThirdPhase)

Services:

        EDC: Yes

        eDiary/ePRO: N/A

        IVRS: N/A

        Mobile Devices: N/A

Web Site: http://www.cmedltd.com

Mailing Address: Holmwood,   Broadlands   Business Campus, Langhurstwood Road, Horsham RH12 4QP, UK

Telephone 1:   +44 (0) 140 375 5050

Telephone 2:   N/A

Fax: +44 (0) 140 375 5051

Email: contact@cmedresearch.com

EDC Providers

Country: **United Kingdom**

CRF Inc.

EDC Products: TrialMax®

Services:

EDC:	N/A
eDiary/ePRO:	Yes
IVRS:	N/A
Mobile Devices:	Yes

Web Site: http://www.crfhealth.com/

Mailing Address: 4 Heathfield Terrace, London, W4 4JE United Kingdom

Telephone 1: +44 208 996 4050

Telephone 2: N/A

Fax: +44 208 996 4051

Email: info-uk@crfhealth.com

Country: **United Kingdom**

CSS Informatics

EDC Products: Oracle Clinical, Clintrial

Services:

EDC:	Yes
eDiary/ePRO:	N/A
IVRS:	N/A
Mobile Devices:	N/A

Web Site: htpp://www.csscomp.com/

Mailing Address: Granta Park, Great Abington, Cambridge CB1 6GQ, United Kingdom

Telephone 1: +44 (0) 122 337 4100

Telephone 2: N/A

Fax: +44 (0) 122 337 4137

Email: infinfo@europe.ppdi.com

EDC Providers

Country: **United Kingdom**

Datatrial Limited

EDC Products: nowEDC™

Services:

EDC:	Yes
eDiary/ePRO:	N/A
IVRS:	N/A
Mobile Devices:	N/A

Web Site: http://www.datatrial.com/

Mailing Address: Mikasa House, Asama Court, Newcastle Business Park, Newcastle upon Tyne, NE4 7YD, UK

Telephone 1:   +44 (0) 191 226 3500

Telephone 2:   N/A

Fax: +44 (0) 191 226 3501

Email: information@datatrial.com

Country: **United Kingdom**

eResearch Technology Limited

EDC Products: EXPeRT eClinical, EXPeRT ePRO™

Services:

EDC:	Yes
eDiary/ePRO:	Yes
IVRS:	N/A
Mobile Devices:	N/A

Web Site: http://www.ert.com

Mailing Address: Pegasus House, Bakewell Road, Orton Southgate,Peterborough, Cambridgeshire PE2 6YS, United Kingdom

Telephone 1: +44 (0) 173 3374800

Telephone 2: N/A

Fax: +44 (0) 173 323 8782

Email: eresearch@ert.com

Country: **United Kingdom**

etrials Worldwide, Inc.,

EDC Products: etrials EDC, etrials eDiary, etrials IVR, etrials Integrated Solutions

Services:

EDC:	Yes
eDiary/ePRO:	Yes
IVRS:	Yes
Mobile Devices:	N/A

Web Site: http://www.etrials.com

Mailing Address: Building 735, Kent Science Park, Broad Oak Road, Sittingbourne, Kent, ME9 8GU, UK

Telephone 1: +44 (0) 179 547 9041

Telephone 2: N/A

Fax: +44 (0) 179 547 0528

Email: N/A

Country: **United Kingdom**

Formedix

EDC Products: Formedix Origin, Formedix Transform

Services:

EDC:	Yes
eDiary/ePRO:	N/A
IVRS:	N/A
Mobile Devices:	N/A

Web Site: http://www.formedix.com

Mailing Address: Suite 2010, Mile End, Abbey Mill, Seedhill, Paisley, PA1 1JS, UK

Telephone 1: +44 (0) 141 561 4150

Telephone 2: N/A

Fax: +44 (0) 800 781 6192

Email: wecanhelp@formedix.com

Country: **United Kingdom**

Harrison Clinical Research Limited

EDC Products: Marvin

Services:

EDC:	Yes
eDiary/ePRO:	Yes
IVRS:	N/A
Mobile Devices:	N/A

Web Site: http://www.harrisonclinical.com

Mailing Address: Gemini House, Bartholomew's Walk, Cambridgeshire Business Park, Angel Drove, Ely, Cambridgeshire, CB7 4EA, UK

Telephone 1: +44 (0) 135 366 8339

Telephone 2: N/A

Fax: +44 (0) 135 366 1580

Email: N/A

Country: **United Kingdom**

Health Decisions Ltd.

<u>EDC Products:</u> SmartPen™, Optical Mark Read (OMR) forms, Web-based EDC, Web-DQS

<u>Services:</u>

EDC:	Yes
eDiary/ePRO:	Yes
IVRS:	Yes
Mobile Devices:	Yes

<u>Web Site:</u> http://www.healthdec.com/

<u>Mailing Address:</u> Windrush Court, Unit J, Abingdon Business Park, Abingdon, OX14 1SY, UK

<u>Telephone 1:</u> +44 (0) 123 555 5111

<u>Telephone 2:</u> N/A

<u>Fax:</u> +44 (0) 123 546 2540

<u>Email:</u> N/A

Country: **United Kingdom**

ICON Clinical Research

EDC Products: Medidata Rave™

Services:

EDC:	Yes
eDiary/ePRO:	N/A
IVRS:	N/A
Mobile Devices:	N/A

Web Site: htpp://www.iconclinical.com/

Mailing Address: Concept House, 6 Stoneycroft Rise, Chandlers Ford, Eastleigh, Hampshire, SO53 3LD, UK

Telephone 1:   +44 238 068 8500

Telephone 2:   N/A

Fax: +44 238 068 8501

Email: N/A

Country: **United Kingdom**

InferMed

<u>**EDC Products:**</u> MACRO

<u>**Services:**</u>

EDC:	Yes
eDiary/ePRO:	N/A
IVRS:	N/A
Mobile Devices:	N/A

<u>**Web Site:**</u> http://www.infermed.com/

<u>**Mailing Address:**</u> 25 Bedford Square, London, WC1B 3W, UK

<u>**Telephone 1:**</u> +44 (0) 20 7291 7410

<u>**Telephone 2:**</u> N/A

<u>**Fax:**</u> +44 (0) 207 291 7489

<u>**Email:**</u> infermed@infermed.com

EDC Providers

Country: **United Kingdom**

Invivodata, Ltd.

<u>EDC Products:</u> DiaryPRO®, SitePRO®, EPX™ ePRO Management System,ePRO-EDC Integration with Medidata Rave®

<u>Services:</u>

EDC:	Yes
eDiary/ePRO:	Yes
IVRS:	N/A
Mobile Devices:	Yes

<u>Web Site:</u> http://www.invivodata.com/

<u>Mailing Address:</u> Queens House, Holly Road, Twickenham TW1 4EG, UK

<u>Telephone 1:</u> +44 (0) 208 823 9590

<u>Telephone 2:</u> N/A

<u>Fax:</u> +44 (0) 20 8823 9436

<u>Email:</u> N/A

Country: **United Kingdom**

Logos Technologies

<u>EDC Products:</u> ALPHADAS EDC, ALPHADAS Web Portal, SMART Patient Diary CARD

<u>Services:</u>

EDC:	Yes
eDiary/ePRO:	Yes
IVRS:	N/A
Mobile Devices:	Yes

<u>Web Site:</u> http://www.logostechnologies.com/

<u>Mailing Address:</u> 91 Peterborough Road, London SW6 3BU, UK

<u>Telephone 1:</u> +44 (0) 870 747 8900

<u>Telephone 2:</u> N/A

<u>Fax:</u> +44 (0) 870 747 8600

<u>Email:</u> contact@logostechnologies.com

Country: **United Kingdom**

Medidata Solutions

EDC Products: Medidata Rave®

Services:

EDC:	Yes
eDiary/ePRO:	N/A
IVRS:	N/A
Mobile Devices:	N/A

Web Site: http://www.mdsol.com

Mailing Address: Harman House, 1 George Street, Uxbridge UB8 1QQ, United Kingdom

Telephone 1: +44 (0) 189 527 5600

Telephone 2: N/A

Fax: +44 (0) 189 527 5602

Email: N/A

Country: **United Kingdom**

Octagon Research Solutions, Limited

EDC Products: ViewPoint FUSE

Services:

EDC:	Yes
eDiary/ePRO:	N/A
IVRS:	N/A
Mobile Devices:	N/A

Web Site: http://www.octagonresearch.com/

Mailing Address: Buckland House, Dower Mews, 108 High Street, Berkhamsted, Hertfordshire, HP4 2BL, United Kingdom

Telephone 1: +44 (0) 144 286 6887

Telephone 2: N/A

Fax: + 44 (0) 144 287 3177

Email: info@octagonresearch.com

Country: **United Kingdom**

Paragon Biomedical, Inc.

EDC Products: Oracle Clinical® and ClinTrials™

Services:

EDC:	Yes
eDiary/ePRO:	N/A
IVRS:	Yes
Mobile Devices:	N/A

Web Site: http://www.parabio.com

Mailing Address: Planar House, Globe Park, Marlow, Bucks, SL7 1YL, UK

Telephone 1: +44 (0) 162 840 2430

Telephone 2: N/A

Fax: +44 (0) 162 847 7125

Email: info@paragonbiomedical.com

Country: **United Kingdom**

Perceptive Informatics, UK Ltd.

<u>EDC Products:</u> Perceptive Voice™, ALADDIN™, ePRO

<u>Services:</u>

EDC:	N/A
eDiary/ePRO:	Yes
IVRS:	Yes
Mobile Devices:	N/A

<u>Web Site:</u>   http://www.perceptive.com/

<u>Mailing Address:</u> River Court, The Quays, 101-105 Oxford Road, Uxbridge UB8 1LZ, United Kingdom

<u>Telephone 1:</u>   +44 189 523 8000

<u>Telephone 2:</u>   N/A

<u>Fax:</u>   +44 189 523 8494

<u>Email:</u>   info@perceptive.com

Country: **United Kingdom**

Phase Forward Europe Ltd

EDC Products: InForm™, Clintrial™, WebSDM™

Services:

EDC:	Yes
eDiary/ePRO:	N/A
IVRS:	N/A
Mobile Devices:	N/A

Web Site: http://www.phaseforward.com

Mailing Address: 2nd Floor, Voyager Place, Shoppenhangers Road, Maidenhead, Berkshire, SL6 2PJ, England

Telephone 1: +44 (0) 162 864 0700

Telephone 2: N/A

Fax: +44 (0) 162 877 9031

Email: info.europe@phaseforward.com

PPD

EDC Products: Acceliant eClinical Suite, Oracle Clinical
Remote Data Capture

Services:

EDC:	Yes
eDiary/ePRO:	N/A
IVRS:	Yes
Mobile Devices:	N/A

Web Site: http://www.ppdi.com/

Mailing Address: Avondale House, Phoenix Crescent,
Strathclyde Business Park, Bellshill, Lanarkshire,
ML4 3NJ, UK

Telephone 1: +44 169 846 4390

Telephone 2: N/A

Fax: +44 169 846 4391

Email: N/A

Premier Research

EDC Products: Oracle Clinical Remote Data Capture

Services:

EDC:	Yes
eDiary/ePRO:	N/A
IVRS:	N/A
Mobile Devices:	N/A

Web Site: http://www.premier-research.com

Mailing Address: 30 Wellington Business Park, Dukes Ride, Crowthorne, Berkshire, RG45 6LS, United Kingdom

Telephone 1: +44 (0) 134 475 2375

Telephone 2: N/A

Fax: +44 (0) 134 475 2374

Email: N/A

Country: **United Kingdom**

Quadratek Data Solutions Ltd.

EDC Products: Clincase

Services:

EDC:	Yes
eDiary/ePRO:	N/A
IVRS:	N/A
Mobile Devices:	N/A

Web Site: http://www.quadratek.net

Mailing Address: Quadratek House, 1 Farnham Road, Guildford, Surrey, GU2 4RG, United Kingdom

Telephone 1: +44 (0) 870 428 9039

Telephone 2: N/A

Fax: +44 (0) 148 354 9100

Email: N/A

Country: **United Kingdom**

Quintegra Solutions Limited

EDC Products: Quintegra's CDMS

Services:

EDC:	Yes
eDiary/ePRO:	N/A
IVRS:	N/A
Mobile Devices:	N/A

Web Site: htpp://www.quintegrasolutions.com/

Mailing Address: Regent House, 24-25 Nut ford Place, London, W1H 5YN, UK

Telephone 1: +44 207 569 3039

Telephone 2: N/A

Fax: +44 207 569 3001

Email: N/A

Country: **United Kingdom**

StudyBuilder UK

EDC Products: StudyBuilder

Services:

EDC:	Yes
eDiary/ePRO:	Yes
IVRS:	N/A
Mobile Devices:	Yes

Web Site: www.studybuilder.co.uk

Mailing Address: John Eccles House, Robert Robinson Avenue, The Oxford Science Park, OX4 4GP, United Kingdom

Telephone 1: +44 186 533 8092

Telephone 2: 0 186 533 8092

Fax: 0 186 533 8100

Email: uk@studybuilder.com

Country: **United Kingdom**

Syne qua non Ltd

EDC Products: Syneclin

Services:

EDC:	Yes
eDiary/ePRO:	N/A
IVRS:	N/A
Mobile Devices:	N/A

Web Site: http://www.synequanon.com

Mailing Address: Navire House, Mere Street, Diss, Norfolk, IP22 4AG, UK

Telephone 1:   +44 (0) 137 964 4449

Telephone 2:   N/A

Fax: +44 (0) 137 964 4445

Email: sqn@synequanon.com

Country: **United Kingdom**

Tessella Inc.

EDC Products: Adaptive Clinical Trials

Services:

EDC:	Yes
eDiary/ePRO:	Yes
IVRS:	N/A
Mobile Devices:	Yes

Web Site: http://www.tessella.com/

Mailing Address: 3 Vineyard Chambers, Abingdon, Oxfordshire, OX14 3PX, UK

Telephone 1: +44 (0) 123 555 5511

Telephone 2: N/A

Fax: +44 (0) 123 555 3301

Email: nfo@tessella.com

Country: **United Kingdom**

United Biosource Corporation

<u>EDC Products:</u> ClinPlus® Data Management System, SAS®-based

<u>Services:</u>

EDC:	Yes
eDiary/ePRO:	Yes
IVRS:	Yes
Mobile Devices:	Yes

<u>Web Site:</u> http://www.unitedbiosource.com

<u>Mailing Address:</u> 20 Bloomsbury Square, London WC1A 2NS, UK

<u>Telephone 1:</u> +44 207 299 4550

<u>Telephone 2:</u> N/A

<u>Fax:</u>   +44 207 299 4555

<u>Email:</u>   analytics@unitedbiosource.com

USA

AAIPharma Inc.

EDC Products: multiple EDC platforms

Services:

EDC: Yes

eDiary/ePRO: N/A

IVRS: N/A

Mobile Devices: N/A

Web Site: http://www.aaipharma.com/

Mailing Address: 2320 Scientific Park Drive, Wilmington, North Carolina 28405, USA

Telephone 1: +1 800 575 4224

Telephone 2: N/A

Fax: N/A

Email: services@aaipharma.com

Country: **USA**

Acumen Healthcare Solutions, LLC

EDC Products: TracIt2k

Services:

EDC:	Yes
eDiary/ePRO:	N/A
IVRS:	N/A
Mobile Devices:	N/A

Web Site: http://www.acumenhealthcare.com

Mailing Address: 14252 23rd Avenue North, Plymouth, MN 55447, USA

Telephone 1: +1 763 559 8232

Telephone 2: N/A

Fax: +1 763 559 2821

Email: sales@acumenhealthcare.com

Adapt-EDC

EDC Products: ADAPT~EDC

Services:

EDC:	Yes
eDiary/ePRO:	N/A
IVRS:	N/A
Mobile Devices:	N/A

Web Site: http://www.adaptedc.com/

Mailing Address: 5872 York Road, P.O. Box 663, Lahaska, PA 18931, USA

Telephone 1: +1 215 794 5691

Telephone 2: N/A

Fax: N/A

Email: info@adaptedc.com

Country: **USA**

Adobe Systems Incorporated

<u>EDC Products:</u> Adobe LiveCycle ES

<u>Services:</u>

EDC:	Yes
eDiary/ePRO:	N/A
IVRS:	N/A
Mobile Devices:	N/A

<u>Web Site:</u>
http://www.adobe.com/lifesciences/solutions/live cycle/

<u>Mailing Address:</u> 345 Park Avenue,San Jose, CA 95110-2704, USA

<u>Telephone 1:</u> +1 408 536 6000

<u>Telephone 2:</u> N/A

<u>Fax:</u>   +1 408 537 6000

<u>Email:</u>   Use   website   for   communication

Advanced Clinical Research Services, LLC

EDC Products: SurePoint™, Oracle Clinical, Clintrial

Services:

EDC:	Yes
eDiary/ePRO:	N/A
IVRS:	N/A
Mobile Devices:	N/A

Web Site: http://www.ACRXS.com/

Mailing Address: 1200 Lakeside Drive, Bannockburn, IL 60015, USA

Telephone 1: +1 847 267 1176

Telephone 2: N/A

Fax: +1 847 267 1432

Email: N/A

Country: **USA**

Advanced Clinical Software

EDC Products: StudyManager SE, StudyManager EDC

Services:

EDC:	Yes
eDiary/ePRO:	N/A
IVRS:	N/A
Mobile Devices:	N/A

Web Site: http://www.clinicalsoftware.net

Mailing Address: 520 Pike Street, Suite 2522, Seattle, WA 98101, USA

Telephone 1: +1 206 728 0313

Telephone 2: N/A

Fax: +1 206 728 0469

Email: hello@StudyManager.com

Country: **USA**

Afferenz

<u>EDC Products:</u> Acceliant Data Management, MedStudio

<u>Services:</u>

EDC:	Yes
eDiary/ePRO:	N/A
IVRS:	N/A
Mobile Devices:	N/A

<u>Web Site:</u>   http://www.afferenz.com/

<u>Mailing Address:</u> 52 King Street, Watertown, MA 02472, USA

<u>Telephone 1:</u>   +1 617 923 1354

<u>Telephone 2:</u>   N/A

<u>Fax:</u>   N/A

<u>Email:</u>   afferenz-info@megasoft.com

Country: **USA**

Akaza Research

EDC Products: OpenClinica

Services:

EDC:	Yes
eDiary/ePRO:	N/A
IVRS:	N/A
Mobile Devices:	N/A

Web Site: http://www.openclinica.org

Mailing Address: One Kendall Square, Bldg. 400, 4th Floor, Cambridge, MA 02139, USA

Telephone 1: +1 617 621 8585

Telephone 2: N/A

Fax: +1 617 621 0065

Email: contact@akazaresearch.com

Country: **USA**

Arrowhead Electronic Healthcare

EDC Products: ePRO Log

Services:

EDC:	N/A
eDiary/ePRO:	Yes
IVRS:	N/A
Mobile Devices:	N/A

Web Site: http://www.arrowheadehealth.com/

Mailing Address: 260 Addie Roy Rd., Suite 206, Austin, TX 78746-4122, USA

Telephone 1: +1 512 652 0260

Telephone 2: N/A

Fax: +1 512 732 2238

Email: info@aheh.com

Beardsworth Consulting Group, Inc.

EDC Products: BNet3

Services:

        EDC: Yes

        eDiary/ePRO: N/A

        IVRS: N/A

        Mobile Devices: N/A

Web Site: http://www.beardsworth.com

Mailing Address: 70 Church Street, Flemington, NJ 08822, USA

Telephone 1:   +1 800 788 6046

Telephone 2:   N/A

Fax: +1 908 788 5281

Email: info@Beardsworth.com

Biopharm Systems, Inc.

EDC Products: Simple Forms™

Services:

    EDC: Yes

    eDiary/ePRO: N/A

    IVRS: N/A

    Mobile Devices: N/A

Web Site: http://www.biopharm.com

Mailing Address: 2000 Alameda de las Pulgas, Suite 154, San Mateo, CA 94403-1270, USA

Telephone 1: +1 650 292 5300

Telephone 2: N/A

Fax: +1 650 292 5301

Email: info@biopharm.com

Country: **USA**

BioStat Solutions, Inc

EDC Products: Matrix2

Services:

EDC:	Yes
eDiary/ePRO:	N/A
IVRS:	N/A
Mobile Devices:	N/A

Web Site: htpp://www.biostat-solutions.com/

Mailing Address: 5 Ridgeside Court, Suite 202, Mt. Airy, MD 21771 USA

Telephone 1: +1 301 829 4001

Telephone 2: N/A

Fax: +1 301 829 4166

Email: statconsult@biostat-solutions.com

Chiltern International Limited

EDC Products: Not specified

Services:

EDC: Yes

eDiary/ePRO: N/A

IVRS: N/A

Mobile Devices: N/A

Web Site: http://www2.chiltern.com/

Mailing Address: 1241 Volunteer Parkway, Suite 950, Bristol, TN 37620, USA

Telephone 1: +1 423 968 9533

Telephone 2: N/A

Fax: +1 423 968 3567

Email: N/A

Clarix

<u>**EDC Products:**</u> Clarix EDC, Clarix IVRS

<u>**Services:**</u>

EDC:	Yes
eDiary/ePRO:	Yes
IVRS:	Yes
Mobile Devices:	N/A

<u>**Web Site:**</u>   http://www.clarixinformatics.com

<u>**Mailing Address:**</u> Two Radnor Corporate Center, Radnor, PA 19087, USA

<u>**Telephone 1:**</u>   +1 610 964 9604

<u>**Telephone 2:**</u>   N/A

<u>**Fax:**</u>   +1 610 964 9365

<u>**Email:**</u>   information@clarixinformatics.com

Country: **USA**

ClearTrial, LLC

EDC Products: ClearTrial Clinical Trial Operations Planning (CTOP) software suite

Services:

EDC:	Yes
eDiary/ePRO:	N/A
IVRS:	N/A
Mobile Devices:	N/A

Web Site: htpp://www.cleartrial.com/

Mailing Address: 900 Oakmont Lane, Westmont, IL 60559, USA

Telephone 1: +1 630 986 9800

Telephone 2: N/A

Fax: +1 630 986 9801

Email: Use website for communication

ClinicalTrialsNet Inc.

<u>EDC Products:</u> ClinTriNet

<u>Services:</u>

EDC:	Yes
eDiary/ePRO:	N/A
IVRS:	N/A
Mobile Devices:	N/A

<u>Web Site:</u>   http://www.clinicaltrialsnet.com/

<u>Mailing Address:</u> 12 John Street, Charleston, SC 29403, USA

<u>Telephone 1:</u>   +1 843 475 2429

<u>Telephone 2:</u>   N/A

<u>Fax:</u>   +1 843 965 5406

<u>Email:</u>   info@clinicaltrialsnet.com

Clinilabs

EDC Products: a variety of vendors

Services:

EDC:	Yes
eDiary/ePRO:	Yes
IVRS:	N/A
Mobile Devices:	Yes

Web Site: http://www.clinilabs.com

Mailing Address: 423 W. 55th Street / 4th Floor, New York, NY 10019, USA

Telephone 1: +1 646 215 6400

Telephone 2: N/A

Fax: N/A

Email: N/A

Clinimetrics

EDC Products: Oracle™ Clinical Remote Data Capture (RDC)

Services:

EDC:	Yes
eDiary/ePRO:	N/A
IVRS:	N/A
Mobile Devices:	N/A

Web Site: http://www.clinimetrics.com

Mailing Address: 5285 Hellyer Avenue, San Jose, California 95138, USA

Telephone 1: +1 408 452 8215

Telephone 2: N/A

Fax: +1 408 452 0912

Email: N/A

EDC Providers

Country: **USA**

Clinipace

EDC Products: TEMPO

Services:

  EDC: Yes

  eDiary/ePRO: N/A

  IVRS: N/A

  Mobile Devices: N/A

Web Site: http://www.clinipace.com/

Mailing Address: 3200 Chapel Hill- Nelson Blvd, Research Triangle Park, NC 27709, USA

Telephone 1: +1 919 224 8800

Telephone 2: N/A

Fax: N/A

Email: info@clinipace.com

Country: **USA**

ClinPhone Plc.

EDC Products: ClinPhone Combined EDC-IVR: DataLabs by ClinPhone (EDC/CDMS) and ClinPhone IVR/IWR

Services:

EDC:	Yes
eDiary/ePRO:	Yes
IVRS:	Yes
Mobile Devices:	N/A

Web Site: http://www.clinphone.com

Mailing Address: Windsor Corporate Park, 50 Millstone Road, Building 100, Suite 200, East Windsor, NJ 08520, USA

Telephone 1: +1 609 524 4100

Telephone 2: N/A

Fax: +1 609 448 8790

Email: info@clinphone.com

Cmed Inc.

EDC Products: Timaeus (formerly known as ThirdPhase)

Services:

    EDC: Yes

    eDiary/ePRO: N/A

    IVRS: N/A

    Mobile Devices: N/A

Web Site: htpp://www.cmedltd.com/

Mailing Address: 430 Mountain Avenue, 4th Floor, Murray Hill, NJ 07974, USA

Telephone 1: +1 908 665 1090

Telephone 2: N/A

Fax: +1 908 665 9030

Email: contact@cmedresearch.com

Country: **USA**

CompleWare Corporation

<u>EDC Products:</u> ClinDataLink, crfWorldLink, HomeCDL, HomeCDL-Online, RandomizeIT, ScanCRF, SymptomPhoneLink, SymptomScoreCardII, WebCDL, WebCRF, WebEPRO, CompleClinical Suite

<u>Services:</u>

EDC:	Yes
eDiary/ePRO:	Yes
IVRS:	Yes
Mobile Devices:	Yes

<u>Web Site:</u>   http://www.compleware.com/

<u>Mailing Address:</u> 2865 Stoner Court, North Liberty, IA 52317, USA

<u>Telephone 1:</u>   +1 319 626 8888

<u>Telephone 2:</u>   +1 800 369 8888

<u>Fax:</u>   +1 319 626 8750

<u>Email:</u>   info@compleware.com

CRF Inc.

EDC Products: TrialMax®

Services:

EDC: N/A

eDiary/ePRO: Yes

IVRS: N/A

Mobile Devices: Yes

Web Site: http://www.crfhealth.com/

Mailing Address: 504 Totten Pond Rd., Waltham, MA 02451, USA

Telephone 1: +1 781 250 4400

Telephone 2: N/A

Fax: +1 781 250 2830

Email: info-us@crfhealth.com

Criterium, Inc.

EDC Products: StudyControl™

Services:

        EDC: Yes

        eDiary/ePRO: N/A

        IVRS: Yes

        Mobile Devices: N/A

Web Site: http://www.criteriuminc.com

Mailing Address: Criterium Headquarters, 358 Broadway, Suite 201, Saratoga Springs, NY 12866, USA

Telephone 1:   +1 518 583 0095

Telephone 2:   N/A

Fax: +1 518 583 0394

Email: N/A

Country: **USA**

CSS Informatics

EDC Products: Oracle Clinical, Clintrial

Services:

EDC:	Yes
eDiary/ePRO:	N/A
IVRS:	N/A
Mobile Devices:	N/A

Web Site: htpp://www.csscomp.com/

Mailing Address: 84 Sherman Street, Cambridge, MA 02140, USA

Telephone 1: +1 617 868 6878

Telephone 2: N/A

Fax: +1 617 868 2654

Email: swong@csscomp.com

EDC Providers

Country: **USA**

Databean, LLC

EDC Products: TrialPoint™EDC

Services:

EDC:	Yes
eDiary/ePRO:	N/A
IVRS:	N/A
Mobile Devices:	N/A

Web Site: http://www.databean.com/

Mailing Address: 1441 Route 22, Suite 202, Brewster NY 10509, USA

Telephone 1: +1 845 278 0576

Telephone 2: N/A

Fax: +1 866 210 2529

Email: N/A

DATATRAK International, Inc.

EDC Products: eClinical

Services:

      EDC: Yes

      eDiary/ePRO: Yes

      IVRS: Yes

      Mobile Devices: N/A

Web Site: http://www.datatrak.net

Mailing Address: 6150 Parkland Blvd., Suite 100, Mayfield Heights, OH 44124, USA

Telephone 1:   +1 888 677 DATA (3282)

Telephone 2:   +1 440 443 0082

Fax: +1 440 442 3482

Email: company@datatrak.net

Country: **USA**

Datatrial Limited

EDC Products: nowEDC™

Services:

EDC:	Yes
eDiary/ePRO:	N/A
IVRS:	N/A
Mobile Devices:	N/A

Web Site: http://www.datatrial.com/

Mailing Address: Suite 215, Smoketree Tower, 3100 Smoketree Court, Raleigh, North Carolina, 27604, USA

Telephone 1: +1 919 277 0050

Telephone 2: N/A

Fax: +1 866 220 8614

Email: information@datatrial.com

Country: **USA**

DSG

EDC Products: eCaseLink EDC, eDiaryLink ePRO

Services:

EDC:	Yes
eDiary/ePRO:	Yes
IVRS:	N/A
Mobile Devices:	Yes

Web Site: http://www.dsg-us.com

Mailing Address: 325 Technology Drive, Malvern, PA 19355, USA

Telephone 1: +1 484 913 0210

Telephone 2: N/A

Fax: +1 484 913 0224

Email: info@dsg-us.com

DZS Software Solutions, Inc.

EDC Products: ClinPlus® Data Management (CPDM), SAS based

Services:

EDC:	Yes
eDiary/ePRO:	N/A
IVRS:	N/A
Mobile Devices:	N/A

Web Site: http://www.clinplus.com/

Mailing Address: 1661 Route 22 West, Bound Brook, NJ 08805, USA

Telephone 1: +1 732 764 6969

Telephone 2: +1 866 CLINPLUS

Fax: +1 732 764 6755

Email: salesandmarketing@clinplus.com

Elashoff Consulting

EDC Products: In-house system, based on Microsoft Infopath

Services:

EDC:	Yes
eDiary/ePRO:	N/A
IVRS:	N/A
Mobile Devices:	N/A

Web Site: http://www.elashoffconsulting.com/

Mailing Address:

Telephone 1:   +1 240 988 3040

Telephone 2:   N/A

Fax: N/A

Email: barbara@elashoffconsulting.com

Eliassen Group

EDC Products: Medidata Rave

Services:

EDC:	Yes
eDiary/ePRO:	Yes
IVRS:	N/A
Mobile Devices:	N/A

Web Site: http://www.eliassen.com

Mailing Address: 603 West Street, Mansfield, MA 02048, USA

Telephone 1: +1 508 337 4230

Telephone 2: +1 860 440 6928

Fax: N/A

Email: solutions@eliassen.com

Country: **USA**

EMB Statistical Solutions, LLC

EDC Products: N/A

Services:

      EDC: Yes

      eDiary/ePRO: N/A

      IVRS: N/A

      Mobile Devices: N/A

Web Site: htpp://www.embstats.com/

Mailing Address: 55 Corporate Woods, 9300 West 110th Street, Suite 550, Overland Park, Kansas   66210, USA

Telephone 1:   +1 913 322 6555

Telephone 2:   +1 816 522 6340

Fax: +1 913 322 6559

Email: bbishop@EMBstats.com

EDC Providers

Country: **USA**

EMMES

EDC Products: EMMES AdvantageEDC

Services:

EDC:	Yes
eDiary/ePRO:	N/A
IVRS:	N/A
Mobile Devices:	N/A

Web Site: http://www.emmes.com

Mailing Address: 401 North Washington St., Suite 700, Rockville, MD 20850 USA

Telephone 1: +1 301 251 1161

Telephone 2: N/A

Fax: +1 301 251 1355

Email: info@emmes.com

357

Country: **USA**

eResearchTechnology, Inc.

EDC Products: EXPeRT eClinical, EXPeRT ePRO™

Services:

    EDC: Yes

    eDiary/ePRO: Yes

    IVRS: N/A

    Mobile Devices: N/A

Web Site: http://www.ert.com

Mailing Address: 30 South 17th Street, Philadelphia, PA 19103-4001, USA

Telephone 1:   +1 215 972 0420

Telephone 2:   N/A

Fax: +1 215 972 0414

Email: eresearch@ert.com

Essential Group, Inc.

<u>EDC Products:</u> EssentialSM eStudy

<u>Services:</u>

EDC: Yes

eDiary/ePRO: N/A

IVRS: N/A

Mobile Devices: N/A

<u>Web Site:</u> http://www.essentialgroupinc.com/

<u>Mailing Address:</u> 1325 Tri-State Parkway, Suite 300, Gurnee, IL 60031, USA

<u>Telephone 1:</u> +1 847 855 7676

<u>Telephone 2:</u> +1 888 287 2722

<u>Fax:</u> +1 847 855 9676

<u>Email:</u> sales@essentialgroupinc.com

Country: **USA**

etrials Worldwide, Inc.,

<u>EDC Products:</u> etrials EDC, etrials eDiary, etrials IVR, etrials Integrated Solutions

<u>Services:</u>

EDC:	Yes
eDiary/ePRO:	Yes
IVRS:	Yes
Mobile Devices:	N/A

<u>Web Site:</u> http://www.etrials.com

<u>Mailing Address:</u> Corporate Headquarters:Morrisville Office,4000 Aerial Center Parkway,Morrisville, NC 27560,USA

<u>Telephone 1:</u> +1 919 653 3400

<u>Telephone 2:</u> N/A

<u>Fax:</u> +1 919 653 3620

<u>Email:</u> N/A

ExpeData, LLC

EDC Products: ExpeData Digital Writing Platform (EDWP)

Services:

> **EDC:** N/A
>
> **eDiary/ePRO:** N/A
>
> **IVRS:** N/A
>
> **Mobile Devices:** Yes

Web Site: http://www.expedata.net/

Mailing Address: 600 Albany Street, Dayton, OH 45403, USA

Telephone 1: +1 937 221 1070

Telephone 2: N/A

Fax: N/A

Email: N/A

Formedix

EDC Products: Formedix Origin, Formedix Transform

Services:

EDC:	Yes
eDiary/ePRO:	N/A
IVRS:	N/A
Mobile Devices:	N/A

Web Site: http://www.formedix.com

Mailing Address: 35 Corporate Drive, 4th Floor, Burlington, MA 01803, USA

Telephone 1: +1 781 685 4995

Telephone 2: N/A

Fax: +1 781 685 4601

Email: wecanhelp@formedix.com

Harrison Clinical Research USA

EDC Products: Marvin

Services:

EDC:	Yes
eDiary/ePRO:	Yes
IVRS:	N/A
Mobile Devices:	N/A

Web Site: http://Dr.Pierce1.net

Mailing Address: 5563, Regimental Place, Cincinnati, Ohio 45239, USA

Telephone 1: +1 513 681 4084

Telephone 2: N/A

Fax: +1 513 681 4094

Email: N/A

Health Decisions Inc.

<u>EDC Products:</u> SmartPen™, Optical Mark Read (OMR) forms, Web-based EDC, Web-DQS

<u>Services:</u>

EDC:	Yes
eDiary/ePRO:	Yes
IVRS:	Yes
Mobile Devices:	Yes

<u>Web Site:</u> http://www.healthdec.com/

<u>Mailing Address:</u> 6350 Quadrangle Drive, Suite 300, Chapel Hill, NC 27517, USA

<u>Telephone 1:</u> +1 919 967 1111

<u>Telephone 2:</u> N/A

<u>Fax:</u> +1 919 967 1145

<u>Email:</u> N/A

Healthcare Technology Systems, Inc.

EDC Products: N/A

Services:

EDC: N/A

eDiary/ePRO: N/A

IVRS: Yes

Mobile Devices: N/A

Web Site: http://www.healthtechsys.com/

Mailing Address: 7617 Mineral Point Road, Suite 300, Madison, WI 53717, USA

Telephone 1: +1 608 827 2440

Telephone 2: N/A

Fax: +1 608 827 2444

Email: sales@healthtechsys.com

Country: **USA**

i3 Statprobe

EDC Products: Oracle® Clinical Remote Data Capture (OC RDC)

Services:

EDC:	Yes
eDiary/ePRO:	N/A
IVRS:	N/A
Mobile Devices:	N/A

Web Site:
http://www.i3global.com/Businesses/i3Statprobe/

Mailing Address: Locations: US-NC-Cary, US-CA-San Diego, US-MI-Ann Arbor, US-MN-Eden Prairie, US-NJ-Basking Ridge, US-TX-Austin

Telephone 1: +1 866 427 6848

Telephone 2: +1 801 982 3402

Fax: N/A

Email: info@i3global.com

Country: **USA**

ICON Clinical Research

EDC Products: Medidata Rave™

Services:

EDC:	Yes
eDiary/ePRO:	N/A
IVRS:	N/A
Mobile Devices:	N/A

Web Site: htpp://www.iconclinical.com/

Mailing Address: 212 Church Road, North Wales, PA 19454, USA

Telephone 1: +1 215 616 3000

Telephone 2: N/A

Fax: +1 215 699 6288

Email: info@iconus.com

iMedRIS Data Corporation

EDC Products: iRIS™

Services:

EDC:	Yes
eDiary/ePRO:	N/A
IVRS:	N/A
Mobile Devices:	N/A

Web Site: htpp://www.imedris.com/

Mailing Address: 625 E. Carnegie Dr., Suite 105, San Bernardino, CA 92408, USA

Telephone 1: +1 909 890 2224

Telephone 2: N/A

Fax: +1 909 890 2498

Email: info@imedris.com

InforMedix, Inc.

<u>EDC Products:</u> The Med-eMonitor™ System

<u>Services:</u>

EDC: N/A

eDiary/ePRO: Yes

IVRS: N/A

Mobile Devices: Yes

<u>Web Site:</u>   htpp://www.informedix.com/

<u>Mailing Address:</u> Georgetowne Park, 5880 Hubbard Drive, Rockville, MD 20852, USA

<u>Telephone 1:</u>   +1 301 984 1566

<u>Telephone 2:</u>   N/A

<u>Fax:</u>   N/A

<u>Email:</u>   info@informedix.com

Country: **USA**

Innovative Clinical Research Solutions

EDC Products: Acquire EDC

Services:

EDC:	Yes
eDiary/ePRO:	N/A
IVRS:	N/A
Mobile Devices:	N/A

Web Site: http://icrs.rfmh.org/

Mailing Address: 140 Old Orangeburg Road, Orangeburg, NY 10962, USA

Telephone 1: +1 845 398 6514

Telephone 2: N/A

Fax: +1 845 398 6509

Email: N/A

Invivodata, Inc.

EDC Products: DiaryPRO®, SitePRO®, EPX™ ePRO Management System,ePRO-EDC Integration with Medidata Rave®

Services:

EDC:	Yes
eDiary/ePRO:	Yes
IVRS:	N/A
Mobile Devices:	Yes

Web Site: http://www.invivodata.com/

Mailing Address: 2100 Wharton Street, Suite 505, Pittsburgh, PA 15203, USA

Telephone 1: +1 412 390 3000

Telephone 2: N/A

Fax: +1 412 390 3020

Email: N/A

IVR Clinical Concepts

EDC Products: IVRCC's Electronic Patient Diaries

Services:

EDC: N/A

eDiary/ePRO: Yes

IVRS: Yes

Mobile Devices: N/A

Web Site: http://www.ivrcc.com/

Mailing Address: 600 S. Dixie Hwy., Suite 202, Boca Raton , FL 33432, USA

Telephone 1: +1 800 486 1779

Telephone 2: +1 561 705 1986

Fax: N/A

Email: N/A

IVRESS, LLC

EDC Products: IVRESS

Services:

EDC:	N/A
eDiary/ePRO:	Yes
IVRS:	Yes
Mobile Devices:	N/A

Web Site: http://www.ivress.com/

Mailing Address: 2 Nighthawk Street, Hilton Head Island, SC 29928, USA

Telephone 1:   +1 843 842 7379

Telephone 2:   N/A

Fax: +1 843 842 9906

Email: info@ivress.com

Country: **USA**

KIKA Medical, Inc.

EDC Products: Eventa™

Services:

    EDC: Yes

    eDiary/ePRO: N/A

    IVRS: N/A

    Mobile Devices: N/A

Web Site: http://www.kikamedical.com/

Mailing Address: 21 Milk Street - 5th Floor, Boston, MA 02109, USA

Telephone 1:   +1 617 619 9990

Telephone 2:   N/A

Fax: +1 617 422 0854

Email: sales-us@kikamedical.com

Kronos Communicated Data, Inc.

EDC Products: the Kronos System

Services:

EDC:	Yes
eDiary/ePRO:	Yes
IVRS:	Yes
Mobile Devices:	Yes

Web Site: http://www.kronosdata.com/

Mailing Address: 456 North Tamiami Trail, Sarasota, FL 34229, USA

Telephone 1:   +1 888 538 1690

Telephone 2:   +1 941 966 1400

Fax: +1 941 966 6191

Email: kronos@kronosdata.com

LifeTree eClinical

EDC Products: LifeTree ICTM™

Services:

EDC:	Yes
eDiary/ePRO:	N/A
IVRS:	N/A
Mobile Devices:	N/A

Web Site: http://www.lifetreeeclinical.com

Mailing Address: 41093 County Center Drive, Temecula, CA 92591, USA

Telephone 1: +1 800 211 2799

Telephone 2: N/A

Fax: +1 877 659 5433

Email: info@lifetree-tech.com

Maaguzi

EDC   Products: OutcomeLogix Data Capture, OutcomeLogix ePro

Services:

EDC:	Yes
eDiary/ePRO:	Yes
IVRS:	N/A
Mobile Devices:	Yes

Web Site: http://www.maaguzi.com/

Mailing Address: 11711 N Meridian Street, Suite 580, Carmel, IN 46032, USA

Telephone 1: +1 317 815 1983

Telephone 2: N/A

Fax: N/A

Email: info@maaguzi.com

Majaro Infosystems Inc.

EDC Products: ClinAccess™, SAS based

Services:

EDC:	Yes
eDiary/ePRO:	N/A
IVRS:	N/A
Mobile Devices:	N/A

Web Site: http://www.majaro.com/

Mailing Address: 2350 Mission College Blvd., Suite 700, Santa Clara, California 95054, USA

Telephone 1: +1 408 330 9400

Telephone 2: N/A

Fax: +1 408 330 9410

Email: info@majaro.com

Medical Graphics Corporation

EDC Products: BreezeSuite

Services:

EDC:	Yes
eDiary/ePRO:	N/A
IVRS:	N/A
Mobile Devices:	N/A

Web Site: http://www.medgraphics.com/cr/

Mailing Address: 350 Oak Grove Parkway, St. Paul, MN 55127, USA

Telephone 1: +1 651 766 3429

Telephone 2: +1 800 950 5597 ext. 1429

Fax: N/A

Email: clinicalresearch@medgraphics.com

Country: **USA**

Medidata Solutions

EDC Products: Medidata Rave®

Services:

EDC:	Yes
eDiary/ePRO:	N/A
IVRS:	N/A
Mobile Devices:	N/A

Web Site: http://www.mdsol.com

Mailing Address: 79 Fifth Avenue, 8th Floor, New York, New York 10003, USA

Telephone 1: +1 212 918 1800

Telephone 2: +1 877 511 4200

Fax: +1 212 918 1818

Email: N/A

MedNet Solutions, Inc.

<u>EDC Products:</u> MedNet eClinical Solution

<u>Services:</u>

EDC:	Yes
eDiary/ePRO:	N/A
IVRS:	N/A
Mobile Devices:	N/A

<u>Web Site:</u> http://www.mednetstudy.com/

<u>Mailing Address:</u> 601 Carlson Parkway, Suite 605, Minnetonka, MN 55305, USA

<u>Telephone 1:</u> +1 866 258 2735

<u>Telephone 2:</u> +1 763 258 2735

<u>Fax:</u> +1 763 258 2737

<u>Email:</u> contact@mednetstudy.com

Country: **USA**

Medrio

EDC Products: Medrio

Services:

EDC:	Yes
eDiary/ePRO:	N/A
IVRS:	N/A
Mobile Devices:	N/A

Web Site: http://www.medrio.com/

Mailing Address: 1330 Broadway, Suite 831, Oakland, CA 94612, USA

Telephone 1: +1 877 763 3746

Telephone 2: N/A

Fax: N/A

Email: info@medrio.com

MedTrials, Inc.

<u>**EDC Products:**</u> works with a number of qualified EDC vendors

<u>**Services:**</u>

EDC:	Yes
eDiary/ePRO:	N/A
IVRS:	N/A
Mobile Devices:	N/A

<u>**Web Site:**</u>   http://www.medtrials.com/

<u>**Mailing Address:**</u> 2777 Stemmons Freeway, Suite 900, Dallas, TX 75207-2273, USA

<u>**Telephone 1:**</u>   +1 214 630 0288

<u>**Telephone 2:**</u>   N/A

<u>**Fax:**</u>   +1 214 630 0289

<u>**Email:**</u>   careers@medtrials.com

Mi-Co

EDC Products: Mi-Forms

Services:

EDC:	Yes
eDiary/ePRO:	Yes
IVRS:	N/A
Mobile Devices:	Yes

Web Site: http://www.mi-corporation.com

Mailing Address: 2 Davis Drive, P.O. Box 12076, Research Triangle Park, NC 27709, USA

Telephone 1: +1 919 485 4819

Telephone 2: N/A

Fax: +1 919 485 0621

Email: N/A

Country: **USA**

MWI (eCRF+)

EDC Products: e-CRF+

Services:

EDC:	Yes
eDiary/ePRO:	N/A
IVRS:	N/A
Mobile Devices:	N/A

Web Site: http://www.ecrfplus.com/

Mailing Address: N/A

Telephone 1:   +1 425 654 1804

Telephone 2:   N/A

Fax: +1 425 427 6028

Email: info@ecrfplus.com

New England Research Institutes

<u>EDC Products:</u> ADEPT (Advanced Data Entry and Protocol Tracking)

<u>Services:</u>

EDC:	Yes
eDiary/ePRO:	N/A
IVRS:	N/A
Mobile Devices:	N/A

<u>Web Site:</u> http://www.neriscience.com

<u>Mailing Address:</u> 9 Galen Street, Watertown, MA 02472, USA

<u>Telephone 1:</u> +1 617 923 7747

<u>Telephone 2:</u> N/A

<u>Fax:</u> +1 617 926 8246

<u>Email:</u> media@neriscience.com

Nextrials, Inc.

EDC Products: PRISM

Services:

EDC:	Yes
eDiary/ePRO:	N/A
IVRS:	N/A
Mobile Devices:	N/A

Web Site: http://www.nextrials.com

Mailing Address: 5000 Executive Parkway, Suite 540, San Ramon, California 94583, USA

Telephone 1: +1 925 355 3000

Telephone 2: N/A

Fax: +1 925 355 3005

Email: info@nextrials.com

Northrop Grumman Information Technology

EDC Products: CRF WorkManager

Services:

EDC:	Yes
eDiary/ePRO:	N/A
IVRS:	N/A
Mobile Devices:	N/A

Web Site: http://www.it.northropgrumman.com/

Mailing Address: 7575 Colshire Drive, McLean, VA 22102, USA

Telephone 1:   +1 703 556 1000

Telephone 2:   N/A

Fax: N/A

Email: N/A

nSpire Health, Inc.

EDC Products: eSP (Electronic ShortPath)

Services:

EDC:	Yes
eDiary/ePRO:	Yes
IVRS:	N/A
Mobile Devices:	N/A

Web Site: http://www.nspirehealth.com

Mailing Address: 1830 Lefthand Circle, Longmont, CO 80501, USA

Telephone 1: +1 800 574 7374

Telephone 2: +1 303 666 5555

Fax: +1 303 666 5588

Email: sales@nspirehealth.com

Octagon Research Solutions, Inc.

<u>EDC Products:</u> ViewPoint FUSE

<u>Services:</u>

EDC:	Yes
eDiary/ePRO:	N/A
IVRS:	N/A
Mobile Devices:	N/A

<u>Web Site:</u> http://www.octagonresearch.com/

<u>Mailing Address:</u> 779 East Evelyn Avenue, Suite C, Mountain View, CA 94041, USA

<u>Telephone 1:</u> +1 650 230 2355

<u>Telephone 2:</u> N/A

<u>Fax:</u> +1 650 230 2363

<u>Email:</u> info@octagonresearch.com

OmniComm Systems, Inc.

EDC Products: TrialMaster®

Services:

EDC: Yes

eDiary/ePRO: N/A

IVRS: N/A

Mobile Devices: N/A

Web Site: http://www.omnicomm.com

Mailing Address: 2101 West Commercial Blvd. Suite 4000, Ft. Lauderdale, FL 33309, USA

Telephone 1:   +1 954 473 1254

Telephone 2:   N/A

Fax: +1 954 473 1256

Email: info@omnicomm.com

Oracle Corporation

<u>EDC Products:</u> Oracle Clinical, Oracle Remote Data Capture

<u>Services:</u>

EDC:	Yes
eDiary/ePRO:	N/A
IVRS:	N/A
Mobile Devices:	N/A

<u>Web Site:</u>
http://www.oracle.com/industries/life_sciences/index.html

<u>Mailing Address:</u> 500 Oracle Parkway, Redwood Shores, CA 94065, USA

<u>Telephone 1:</u>   +1.800 ORACLE1

<u>Telephone 2:</u>   +1 650 506 7000

<u>Fax:</u>   N/A

<u>Email:</u>   REF-ESUITES_US@oracle.com

Country: **USA**

Outcome Sciences

EDC Products: Outcome System®, Outcome Offline™

Services:

EDC:	Yes
eDiary/ePRO:	Yes
IVRS:	Yes
Mobile Devices:	Yes

Web Site: http://www.outcome.com/

Mailing Address: 201 Broadway, 5th Floor, Cambridge, MA 02139, USA

Telephone 1: +1 617 621 1600

Telephone 2: +1 888 526 6700

Fax: +1 617 621 1620

Email: info@outcome.com

Country: **USA**

Palm Inc.

EDC Products: Diet & Exercise Assistant. Taber's Cyclopedic Medical Dictionary. Nursing Central. Davis's Drug Guide. Palm Diabetic Diary. 5 Minute Clinical Consult. HeathFile Plus. CalorieKing Handheld Diet Diary. Biometric Weight Manager. ER Suite.

Services:

EDC:	N/A
eDiary/ePRO:	Yes
IVRS:	N/A
Mobile Devices:	Yes

Web Site:
http://www.palm.com/us/software/health.html

Mailing Address: 950 W. Maude Ave., Sunnyvale, CA 94085, USA

Telephone 1: +1 800 881 7256

Telephone 2: +1 408 617 7000

Fax: +1 408 617 0100

Email: volumepurchases@store.palm.com

Paragon Biomedical, Inc.

EDC Products: Oracle Clinical® and ClinTrials™

Services:

EDC:	Yes
eDiary/ePRO:	N/A
IVRS:	Yes
Mobile Devices:	N/A

Web Site: http://www.parabio.com

Mailing Address: 9685 Research Drive, Irvine, CA 92618, USA

Telephone 1: +1 949 224 2800

Telephone 2: +1 800 6 PARAGON

Fax: +1 949 224 2811

Email: info@paragonbiomedical.com

Perceptive Informatics, Inc.

<u>EDC Products:</u> Perceptive Voice™, ALADDIN™, ePRO

<u>Services:</u>

EDC:	N/A
eDiary/ePRO:	Yes
IVRS:	Yes
Mobile Devices:	N/A

<u>Web Site:</u> http://www.perceptive.com/

<u>Mailing Address:</u> 200 West Street, Waltham, MA 02451, USA

<u>Telephone 1:</u> +1 781 487 9900

<u>Telephone 2:</u> N/A

<u>Fax:</u> +1 781 768 5512

<u>Email:</u> info@perceptive.com

PerMedics Inc.

EDC Products: Surveyor®EDC

Services:

EDC: Yes

eDiary/ePRO: N/A

IVRS: N/A

Mobile Devices: N/A

Web Site: http://www.permedics.com/

Mailing Address: 1475 S. Victoria Ct. Suite C, San Bernardino, CA 92408, USA

Telephone 1: +1 877 4PerMed

Telephone 2: N/A

Fax: +1 909 478 5016

Email: webmaster@permedics.com

PharmaNet Development Group, Inc.

EDC Products: Oracle Clinical™ and PharmaSoft

Services:

EDC: Yes

eDiary/ePRO: N/A

IVRS: Yes

Mobile Devices: N/A

Web Site: http://www.pharmanet.com/

Mailing Address: 504 Carnegie Center, Princeton, NJ 08540, USA

Telephone 1:   +1 609 951 6800

Telephone 2:   N/A

Fax: +1 609 514 0390

Email: N/A

Country: **USA**

PharmaVigilant

EDC Products: InSpire

Services:

EDC:	Yes
eDiary/ePRO:	N/A
IVRS:	N/A
Mobile Devices:	N/A

Web Site: http://www.pharmavigilant.com/

Mailing Address: 45 Lyman St., Suite 18, Westborough, MA 01581, USA

Telephone 1: +1 508 898 0004

Telephone 2: N/A

Fax: +1 508 898 0005

Email: sales@pharmavigilant.com

Country: **USA**

Phase Forward Incorporated

EDC Products: InForm™, Clintrial™, WebSDM™

Services:

EDC:	Yes
eDiary/ePRO:	N/A
IVRS:	N/A
Mobile Devices:	N/A

Web Site: http://www.phaseforward.com

Mailing Address: 880 Winter Street, Waltham, MA 02451, USA

Telephone 1:   +1 888 703 1122

Telephone 2:   +1 781 890 7878

Fax: +1 781 890 4848

Email: info@phaseforward.com

Phoenix Data Systems, Inc.

EDC Products: PDS Express

Services:

EDC:	Yes
eDiary/ePRO:	N/A
IVRS:	N/A
Mobile Devices:	N/A

Web Site: http://www.phoenixdatasystems.net/

Mailing Address: Phoenix Data Systems, Inc., 901 East 8th Avenue, Suite 201, King of Prussia, PA 19406, USA

Telephone 1: +1 484 928 6000

Telephone 2: +1 866 737 4332

Fax: +1 484 928 6001

Email: info@pdsedc.com

Phoenix Software International

EDC Products: Entrypoint Plus Clinical Trials Software

Services:

EDC:	Yes
eDiary/ePRO:	N/A
IVRS:	N/A
Mobile Devices:	N/A

Web Site: http://www.entrypointplus.com/

Mailing Address: 5200 West Century Boulevard, Suite 800, Los Angeles, CA 90045, USA

Telephone 1: +1 800 962 8888

Telephone 2: +1 919 841 4545

Fax: +1 919 841 4569

Email: JohnBrayman@entrypointplus.com

Country: **USA**

PHT Corporation

EDC Products: ePRO Product Suite: LogPad System,StudyPad System,eSense Sensors, StudyWorks, Study Archive, ePRO Designer.

Services:

EDC:	Yes
eDiary/ePRO:	Yes
IVRS:	N/A
Mobile Devices:	Yes

Web Site: http://www.phtcorp.com

Mailing Address: 500 Rutherford Avenue, Charlestown, MA 02129, USA

Telephone 1: +1 877 360 2901

Telephone 2: +1 617 973 1600

Fax: +1 617 973 1601

Email: N/A

Country: **USA**

PICS INC.

EDC Products: CERTAS

Services:

EDC:	Yes
eDiary/ePRO:	Yes
IVRS:	Yes
Mobile Devices:	Yes

Web Site: http://certas.com/

Mailing Address: 12007 Sunrise Valley Drive, Suite 480, Reston, VA 20191, USA

Telephone 1: +1 800 543 3744

Telephone 2: +1 703 758 1400

Fax: +1 703 758 1799

Email: N/A

PPD, Inc.

EDC Products: Acceliant eClinical Suite, Oracle Clinical
Remote Data Capture

Services:

EDC:	Yes
eDiary/ePRO:	N/A
IVRS:	Yes
Mobile Devices:	N/A

Web Site: http://www.ppdi.com/

Mailing Address: 929 North Front Street, Wilmington, NC 28401-3331, USA

Telephone 1: +1 910 251 0081

Telephone 2: N/A

Fax: +1 910 762 5820

Email: N/A

Prelude Dynamics, LLC

EDC Products: VISION

Services:

      EDC: Yes

      eDiary/ePRO: N/A

      IVRS: N/A

      Mobile Devices: N/A

Web Site: http://www.preludedynamics.com/

Mailing Address: 815 Brazos Street, Suite 204, Austin, Texas 78701, USA

Telephone 1:   +1 512 476 5100

Telephone 2:   N/A

Fax: N/A

Email: info@preludedynamics.com

Premier Research

<u>EDC Products:</u> Oracle Clinical Remote Data Capture

<u>Services:</u>

EDC: Yes

eDiary/ePRO: N/A

IVRS: N/A

Mobile Devices: N/A

<u>Web Site:</u> http://www.premier-research.com

<u>Mailing Address:</u> 234 Copeland Street, Quincy, MA 02169, USA

<u>Telephone 1:</u> +1 617 237 1100

<u>Telephone 2:</u> N/A

<u>Fax:</u> +1 617 237 1101

<u>Email:</u> N/A

Progressive Life Sciences

<u>EDC Products:</u> In house solutions, combined with OpenClinica, SPSS, EpiInfo

<u>Services:</u>

EDC: Yes

eDiary/ePRO: N/A

IVRS: N/A

Mobile Devices: N/A

<u>Web Site:</u>
htpp://www.progressivelifesciences.com/

<u>Mailing Address:</u> San Jose, CA

<u>Telephone 1:</u> +1 408 694 7632

<u>Telephone 2:</u> N/A

<u>Fax:</u> +1 309 416 2365

<u>Email:</u> info@progressivelifesciences.com

Promedica International

EDC Products: Combined EDC-IVR: DataLabs by ClinPhone (EDC/CDMS) and ClinPhone IVR/IWR

Services:

EDC:	Yes
eDiary/ePRO:	Yes
IVRS:	Yes
Mobile Devices:	N/A

Web Site: http://www.promedica-intl.com

Mailing Address: 3100 Bristol Street, Suite 250, Costa Mesa, CA 92626, USA

Telephone 1:   +1 714 460 7363

Telephone 2:   N/A

Fax: +1 714 460 7364

Email: hr@promedica–intl.com

ProSanos

EDC Products: Accument™

Services:

EDC: Yes

eDiary/ePRO: N/A

IVRS: N/A

Mobile Devices: N/A

Web Site: http://www.prosanos.com/

Mailing Address: 225 Market Street, Suite 502, Harrisburg PA 17101, USA

Telephone 1: +1 717 635 2140

Telephone 2: N/A

Fax: +1 717 635 2575

Email: info_411@prosanos.com

PTC

EDC Products: NetRegulus NetRM

Services:

EDC:	Yes
eDiary/ePRO:	N/A
IVRS:	N/A
Mobile Devices:	N/A

Web Site: http://www.netregulus.com/

Mailing Address: 140 Kendrick Street, Needham, MA 02494, USA

Telephone 1:   +1 781 370 5000

Telephone 2:   +1 781 370 6000

Fax: N/A

Email: N/A

Country: **USA**

Quality Data Services, Inc.

EDC Products: Not specified

Services:

EDC:	Yes
eDiary/ePRO:	N/A
IVRS:	N/A
Mobile Devices:	N/A

Web Site: http://www.qdservices.com

Mailing Address: 2500 Renaissance Blvd, Suite 170, King of Prussia, PA 19406, USA

Telephone 1: +1 610 354 0404

Telephone 2: N/A

Fax: +1 610 354 0402

Email: info@qdservices.com

Quintegra Solutions, Inc.

EDC Products: Quintegra's CDMS

Services:

EDC:	Yes
eDiary/ePRO:	N/A
IVRS:	N/A
Mobile Devices:	N/A

Web Site: htpp://www.quintegrasolutions.com/

Mailing Address: 600 Alexander Road, 3rd Floor, Princeton, NJ 08540, USA

Telephone 1:   +1 609 356 5172

Telephone 2:   N/A

Fax: +1 609 514 0305

Email: N/A

REGISTRAT®, Inc

EDC Products: REGISTRAT EDC, AVT RightFAX, Computer Assisted Telephone Interview (CATI) System, REGISTRAT's IVR

Services:

EDC:	Yes
eDiary/ePRO:	N/A
IVRS:	Yes
Mobile Devices:	N/A

Web Site: http://www.registrat.com

Mailing Address: 2343 Alexandria Drive, Suite 400 , Lexington, KY 40504-3276 USA

Telephone 1: + 1 859 223 4334

Telephone 2: N/A

Fax: +1 859 223 2005

Email: info@registrat.com

SAS Institute Inc.

EDC Products: SAS® Drug Development

Services:

EDC:	Yes
eDiary/ePRO:	N/A
IVRS:	N/A
Mobile Devices:	N/A

Web Site:

http://www.sas.com/industry/pharma/develop/

Mailing Address: 100 SAS Campus Drive, Cary, NC 27513-2414, USA

Telephone 1: +1 919 677 8000

Telephone 2: N/A

Fax: +1 919 677 4444

Email: N/A

Scientific Software Tools

EDC Products: custom software solutions

Services:

EDC:	Yes
eDiary/ePRO:	N/A
IVRS:	N/A
Mobile Devices:	Yes

Web Site: http://www.sstnet.com

Mailing Address: 1023 East Baltimore Pike, Suite 100, Media, PA 19063-5126, USA

Telephone 1: +1 610 891 1640

Telephone 2: N/A

Fax: +1 610 891 8556

Email: sales@sstnet.com

SGS Life Science Services

EDC Products: Phase Forward InForm

Services:

EDC: Yes

eDiary/ePRO: N/A

IVRS: N/A

Mobile Devices: N/A

Web Site: http://www.clinicalresearch.sgs.com

Mailing Address: 12850 Middlebrook Road, Suite 406, Germantown, MD 20874, USA

Telephone 1:   + 1 877 677 2667

Telephone 2:   N/A

Fax: N/A

Email: N/A

Country: **USA**

Sierra Scientific Software Inc.

EDC Products: CRIS

Services:

EDC:	Yes
eDiary/ePRO:	N/A
IVRS:	N/A
Mobile Devices:	N/A

Web Site: http://www.sierraware.net/

Mailing Address: 1300 Clay St., Suite 600, Oakland, CA 94612, USA

Telephone 1: +1 510 655 2441

Telephone 2: N/A

Fax: +1 510 217 3519

Email: info@sierraware.net

Country: **USA**

Sigmasoft International

EDC Products: DMSys®

Services:

EDC:	Yes
eDiary/ePRO:	N/A
IVRS:	N/A
Mobile Devices:	N/A

Web Site: http://www.sigmasoftintl.com/

Mailing Address: N/A

Telephone 1: N/A

Telephone 2: N/A

Fax: N/A

Email: Use website for communication.

StudyBuilder US

EDC Products: StudyBuilder

Services:

EDC:	Yes
eDiary/ePRO:	Yes
IVRS:	N/A
Mobile Devices:	Yes

Web Site: www.studybuilder.us

Mailing Address: Dept. AA1146, PO BOX 618001, Dallas TX 75261-8001, USA

Telephone 1: +44 186 533 8092

Telephone 2: N/A

Fax: +44 186 533 8100

Email: us@studybuilder.com, info@studybuilder.us

Country: **USA**

Symfo

EDC   Products: SymPRO,   SymQOL,   SymVoice, SymEDC, SymPhone

Services:

EDC:	Yes
eDiary/ePRO:	Yes
IVRS:	Yes
Mobile Devices:	Yes

Web Site: http://www.symfo.com/

Mailing Address: 11 Beacon Street, Suite 1230, Boston, MA 02108, USA

Telephone 1: +1 617 577 9484

Telephone 2: N/A

Fax: N/A

Email: symfo-us@symfo.com

Synteract, Inc.

EDC Products: SynCapture™, SynCoder™, Clintrial™, DataFax™, Oracle® Adverse Event Reporting System (AERS), Integrated Review™

Services:

EDC:	Yes
eDiary/ePRO:	N/A
IVRS:	Yes
Mobile Devices:	N/A

Web Site: http://www.synteract.com/

Mailing Address: 5759 Fleet Street, Suite 100, Carlsbad, CA 92008, USA

Telephone 1: +1 760 268 8200

Telephone 2: N/A

Fax: N/A

Email: emorgan@synteract.com

TAKE Solutions Inc.

EDC Products: OneClinical, fax CRF based

Services:

EDC: Yes

eDiary/ePRO: N/A

IVRS: N/A

Mobile Devices: N/A

Web Site: http://www.takesolutions.com/

Mailing Address: 600 College Road East, Suite 3500, Princeton, NJ 08540 USA

Telephone 1: +1 919 861 6750

Telephone 2: +1 888 993 1541

Fax: N/A

Email: contact@OneClinical.com

Country: **USA**

Target Health Inc.

EDC Products: Target e*CRF®

Services:

EDC:	Yes
eDiary/ePRO:	N/A
IVRS:	N/A
Mobile Devices:	N/A

Web Site: http://www.targethealth.com/

Mailing Address: 261 Madison Avenue, New York, NY 10016, USA

Telephone 1: +1 212 681 2100

Telephone 2: N/A

Fax: N/A

Email: joycehays@targethealth.com

Tessella Inc.

<u>EDC Products:</u> Adaptive Clinical Trials

<u>Services:</u>

EDC: Yes

eDiary/ePRO: Yes

IVRS: N/A

Mobile Devices: Yes

<u>Web Site:</u> http://www.tessella.com/

<u>Mailing Address:</u> 233 Needham Street, Suite 300, Newton, MA 02464, USA

<u>Telephone 1:</u> +1 617 454 1220

<u>Telephone 2:</u> N/A

<u>Fax:</u> +1 617 454 1001

<u>Email:</u> nfo@tessella.com

The Metadata® Company, LLC

EDC Products: Metadata® Ontology Language and Metadata® Toolset

Services:

EDC:	Yes
eDiary/ePRO:	N/A
IVRS:	N/A
Mobile Devices:	N/A

Web Site: htpp://www.metadata.com/

Mailing Address: 444 West Ocean Blvd., Suite 1600, Long Beach, CA 90802, USA

Telephone 1: +1 562 495 2011

Telephone 2: N/A

Fax: +1 562 495 1654

Email: info@Metadata.com

TranSenda International, LLC

EDC Products: Clinical EDC Manager™

Services:

EDC:	Yes
eDiary/ePRO:	N/A
IVRS:	N/A
Mobile Devices:	N/A

Web Site: http://www.transenda.com/

Mailing Address: 2700 156th Ave NE, Suite 250, Bellevue, Washington 98007, USA

Telephone 1: +1 425 895 1300

Telephone 2: +1 866 895 1300

Fax: +1 425 895 1309

Email: N/A

Country: **USA**

United Biosource Corporation

EDC Products: ClinPlus® Data Management System, SAS®-based

Services:

EDC:	Yes
eDiary/ePRO:	Yes
IVRS:	Yes
Mobile Devices:	Yes

Web Site: http://www.unitedbiosource.com

Mailing Address: 7501 Wisconsin Avenue, Suite 705, Bethesda, MD 20814, USA

Telephone 1: +1 866 458 1096

Telephone 2: N/A

Fax: +1 240 644 0421

Email: info@unitedbiosource.com

Velos Inc.

EDC Products: Velos eResearch

Services:

EDC: Yes

eDiary/ePRO: N/A

IVRS: N/A

Mobile Devices: N/A

Web Site: http://www.velos.com/

Mailing Address: 2201 Walnut Avenue, Suite 208, Fremont, CA 94538, USA

Telephone 1: +1 510 739 4010

Telephone 2: +1 866 237 4449

Fax: +1 510 739 4018

Email: info@velos.com

Country: **USA**

Veristat Inc.

EDC Products: ClinTrial, InForm

Services:

EDC:	Yes
eDiary/ePRO:	N/A
IVRS:	N/A
Mobile Devices:	N/A

Web Site: htpp://www.veristatinc.com/

Mailing Address: 1750 Washington Street, Holliston, MA 01746, USA

Telephone 1: +1 508 429 7340

Telephone 2: N/A

Fax: +1 508 429 5741

Email: hr@veristatinc.com

VIASYS Healthcare Inc.

EDC Products: AM 2 + PEF Meter, AM 1 PEF Meter, VIAPAD eDiary

Services:

EDC:	Yes
eDiary/ePRO:	Yes
IVRS:	N/A
Mobile Devices:	Yes

Web Site: http://www.viasyshealthcare.com/

Mailing Address: 227 Washington Street, Suite 200, Conshohocken, PA 19428, USA

Telephone 1: +1 866 4VIASYS

Telephone 2: +1 610 862 0800

Fax: +1 610 862 0836

Email: N/A

VIASYS Healthcare USA

EDC Products: VIAPAD (eDiary), VIAPEN (Digital pen) and AM2+ (combined eDiary and Home Spirometer). VCS WebPortal.

Services:

EDC:	Yes
eDiary/ePRO:	Yes
IVRS:	N/A
Mobile Devices:	Yes

Web Site: http://www.viasysclinical.com/

Mailing Address: 22745 Savi Ranch Parkway, Yorba Linda, CA 92887-4645, USA

Telephone 1: +1 714 919 3361

Telephone 2: +1 714 919 3361

Fax: N/A

Email:
VCS.Business.development@viasyshc.com

Vitalograph, Inc

<u>EDC Products:</u> Not specified

<u>Services:</u>

EDC:	Yes
eDiary/ePRO:	Yes
IVRS:	N/A
Mobile Devices:	Yes

<u>Web Site:</u> http://www.vitalograph.com

<u>Mailing Address:</u> 13310 W. 99th St., Lenexa, KS 66215, USA

<u>Telephone 1:</u> +1 800 255 6626

<u>Telephone 2:</u> N/A

<u>Fax:</u> +1 913 888 4259

<u>Email:</u> vitcs@vitalograph.com

Wingspan Technology, Inc.

EDC Products: Various vendors' systems

Services:

EDC:	Yes
eDiary/ePRO:	N/A
IVRS:	N/A
Mobile Devices:	N/A

Web Site: http://www.wingspan.com/

Mailing Address: 490 Norristown Rd, Suite 151, Blue Bell, PA 19422, USA

Telephone 1: +1 610 941 6500

Telephone 2: N/A

Fax: +1 866 398 7398

Email: info@wingspantech.com

Country: **USA**

XClinical USA

<u>**EDC Products:**</u> MARVIN

<u>**Services:**</u>

        EDC: Yes

        eDiary/ePRO: N/A

        IVRS: N/A

        Mobile Devices: N/A

<u>**Web Site:**</u>   http://www.xclinical.com

<u>**Mailing Address:**</u> 245 First Street - 18th Floor, Cambridge, MA 02142, USA

<u>**Telephone 1:**</u>   +1 617 444 8756

<u>**Telephone 2:**</u>   N/A

<u>**Fax:**</u>   +1 617 444 8405

<u>**Email:**</u>   USA@xclinical.com

XTrials® Research Services

EDC Products: XTrials® EDC

Services:

EDC:	Yes
eDiary/ePRO:	Yes
IVRS:	N/A
Mobile Devices:	N/A

Web Site: htpp://www.industrydynamics.com/

Mailing Address: Division of Industry Dynamics Associates, Inc., 265 Davidson Ave., Suite 202, Somerset, NJ 08873, USA

Telephone 1: +1 732 805 3434

Telephone 2: N/A

Fax: +1 732 805 3387

Email: information@xtrials.com

www.ingramcontent.com/pod-product-compliance
Lightning Source LLC
Chambersburg PA
CBHW022050210326
41519CB00054B/289